RADICAL SACRIFICE

RADICAL SACRIFICE

TERRY EAGLETON

YALE UNIVERSITY PRESS
NEW HAVEN AND LONDON

For information about this and other Yale University Press publications, please contact:
U.S. Office: sales.press@yale.edu   yalebooks.com
Europe Office: sales@yaleup.co.uk   yalebooks.co.uk

Set in Arno Pro by IDSUK (DataConnection) Ltd
Printed in Great Britain by TJ International, Padstow, Cornwall

Library of Congress Control Number: 2017963163

ISBN 978-0-300-23335-3

A catalogue record for this book is available from the British Library.

10 9 8 7 6 5 4 3 2 1

For the Carmelite Sisters of Thicket Priory

When someone freely embraces the symbols of death, or death itself . . . a great release of power for good can be expected to follow.

Mary Douglas, *Purity and Danger*, 1966

CONTENTS

PREFACE

The chapters of this book are part of a broader project, one that turns on a set of ideas which seem to have become central to my later work: death, tragedy, sacrifice, dispossession and the like. For readers who might find these conceptions rather too gloomy, I should add that there is also a good deal in the study about renewal, transformation and revolution, which I see as the other face of the darker notions I have just listed.

Like some other of my recent works, then, this one broods upon questions not commonly investigated by the political left, and certainly not by its postmodern wing. Love, death, suffering, sacrifice, evil, martyrdom, forgiveness and so on are not exactly modish preoccupations among cultural or political theorists today. They are more usually the concern of theologians; and if I myself do not take the dismissive attitude to theology generally to be found among left-wingers, this is because, through a quirk of upbringing, I happen to know a little about it. I know enough, anyway, to be convinced that a great many secular views of the Judaic and Christian lineages are as grossly prejudiced and abysmally ill-informed as those, say, for whom socialism is simply a matter of the Gulag, or feminism the calamitous consequence of women throwing their natural modesty and decorum to the winds. One of the more polemical aims of this book, then, though one that remains largely implicit, is to show up some of these attitudes for the lamentable travesties they are. When it comes to theology, even the most subtle of secular thinkers are at risk of stumbling into a mire of dreary clichés and risible misconceptions.

It is, in fact, no more strange that one like myself indebted to the Marxist legacy should take an interest in theology than that a liberal or social democrat should take an interest in Stendhal or Flaubert. For Marxism is a theory and practice of historical change, not a vision of human existence, and as such is not intended to have anything particularly arresting to say about evil or mortality, suffering or forgiveness, tragic breakdown or the nature of nihilism. For such questions, one tends rather to have recourse to Dostoevsky or St Paul, Shakespeare or Sebald.

I am grateful to my copy-editor, Charlotte Chapman, for her exceptionally efficient and meticulous work. In this, she maintains the extraordinarily high standards of my previous copy-editor at Yale, the erudite and perspicacious Jenny Roberts. I am also deeply grateful to Timothy Radcliffe OP, who gave the book a splendidly scrupulous reading and made a number of illuminating comments on it. My thanks also go to Sam Dunnett, who proved himself to be an excellent research assistant.

Chapter 1

RADICAL SACRIFICE

SACRIFICE HAS NOT proved the most glamorous of notions in the modern age; it smacks of self-abasement and punitive self-denial. It is what long-suffering wives do for their imperious husbands, maid-servants for their pampered mistresses, nurses and steelworkers for the good of the economy and storm troopers for the Fatherland. An exhausted mother in Edward St Aubyn's novel *Mother's Milk*, her life in pieces and her desires unfulfilled, speaks of 'the tyranny of self-sacrifice'. The notion is redolent of masochism, self-loathing and a morbid antipathy to what makes for life. It begins as an attempt to placate a savage God and culminates in the clarion call of the fascist Fatherland, with its necrophiliac rites and ceremonies of self-oblation. J.M. Coetzee writes in *Life and Times of Michael K* of how someone may be simply 'another brick in the pyramid of sacrifice that someone would eventually climb and stand straddle-legged on top of, roaring and beating his chest and announcing himself emperor of all he surveyed'. G.W.F. Hegel, a thinker sometimes mistakenly thought to take a sanguine view of the human condition, writes, 'Even as we look at history as the slaughter bench on which the

1

happiness of nations, the wisdom of states and the virtue of individuals have been sacrificed, a question also necessarily arises in our thoughts: to what final end have these monstrous sacrifices been made?'[1]

For conventional liberal wisdom, self-fulfilment and self-dispossession are essentially at odds. This is not the case for a more radical outlook. One must take a remarkably indulgent view of humankind, as many a liberal does, to assume that the self can come into its own without that fundamental breaking and refashioning of which sacrifice has been one traditional sign. It would be the equivalent of claiming that the forms of political life we see around us could evolve into a state of justice without any notable degree of turbulence. Those who oppose sacrifice to the mutuality of love forget that any durable version of the latter involves the self-giving typical of the former. There is indeed a species of sacrificial love that involves wreaking violence upon the self. The problem is to refuse this death-dealing ideology while recognising with Hegel that in a more fruitful sense of the term, the inner structure of love is sacrificial in any case – though we are speaking once again of reciprocal self-giving, not of the abject capitulation of one partner to the dominion of the other. As one commentary puts it, 'sacrifice and self-denial are not a goal in themselves but the substance of forgetting one's own [self] in loving the other'.[2] 'Forgetting' is a questionable claim, given that love enhances the self in the very act of decentring it. Even so, it provides a useful corrective to the fashionable view that sacrifice is necessarily a form of self-mutilation.

That orthodoxy has been well-nigh unanimous in repudiating the concept of sacrifice as barbarous and benighted. In the wake of Thomas Hobbes, for whom the highest moral duty is self-preservation, Ronald Dworkin claims that one's responsibility for others cannot extend to excessive self-sacrifice, given that one's primary obligation is to one's own life. It is a brand of ethics well suited to middle-class suburbia. There is indeed in Dworkin's view a moral duty to come to the aid of others, but only if the difficulties they face are severe, the cost of the assistance is tolerable and those who require such help depend on you in particular to provide it.[3] In similar spirit, John Rawls opposes the idea of sacrifice for the greater good, denying that a loss of freedom for the few can be justified by the welfare of the many.[4] Jürgen Habermas claims that 'rational morality puts its seal on the abolition of sacrifice', no doubt with slain goats rather than the dead of the French Resistance in mind.[5] It is remarkable that when the term 'sacrifice' enters the discussion, the modern liberal mind turns spontaneously to such issues as domestic servitude and death in the cause of military glory, rather than to the career of Constance Markievicz or the death of Malcolm X.

The modern era's scepticism of sacrifice is nowhere more evident than in its uncertain grasp of the notion. By and large, it has come to mean the voluntary relinquishing of what one finds valuable. But renunciation is only one feature of sacrifice, and not always the most prominent. It is true that it can play a major role in the practice. In his classic study *Primitive Culture*, the Victorian anthropologist Edward Burnett Tylor argues that the sacrificial gift is prized by the gods not for itself but as a token of the worshipper's yielding up of something precious. The gift must be part of one's own substance, so that to surrender it exacts a certain cost.[6] Yet it is not obvious that ritual sacrifice is primarily about self-deprivation. You may sacrificially kill a fatted calf not to rob yourself of your prize beast but to pay the gods the most sumptuous tribute you can muster. Sacrifice cannot be reduced to self-denial. The term is a richly layered one – so much so, in fact, that one eminent French scholar has cast doubt on whether the term has much meaning at all.[7] David Janzen is another to question the possibility of a general theory of sacrifice, insisting on how the meaning of the institution shifts from one cultural context to another (indeed from one book of the Hebrew Bible to another), and issuing a rebuke to René Girard, doyen of sacrificial theory, for passing over this vital point.[8]

Ancient Israel had names for different forms of sacrifice, but no name for the institution as such. There is no discernible essence to the custom, which since the dawn of time has fulfilled a striking diversity of functions. It can be anything from a form of celestial bribery[9] ('I'll give you this if you'll give me that') to the act of martyrdom, in which one makes a gift of one's death to others. Sacrifice is a polythetic term, encompassing a range of activities that need have no single feature in common. It has been seen at various times as gift, tribute, covenant, prayer, bargain, gratitude, atonement, adoration, cajolement, celebration, restitution, expiation, sanctification, propitiation, communion, fellowship, purification and discharge of debt. It can involve a redemptive death, a purging of evil, a refusal of death,[10] a dialogue with divinity, a restoration of cosmic order or a prudent investment in order to secure a profitable return. There are those who have regarded it as a rite of passage or reinforcement of patriarchal power, whereas others have found in it a source of social cohesion, a liberation of vital energies, a ritual working through of guilt or trauma or a species of mourning. Giorgio Agamben sees it as a way of providing an ungrounded social existence with an origin and foundation.[11] Walter Burkert's *Homo Necans* treats it among other things as a form of ritual atonement for the slaying of animals.[12] The practice has also been seen as an attempt to win the attention of the gods, a gesture of obedience to the moral law or social code or a token of one's membership of the nation. If some thinkers discern in such rites an attempt to draw the gods nearer, others find in them an effort to fend them off.

For psychoanalytic thought, it is by sacrificial self-repression that the subject first emerges into being, trading its *jouissance* for a certain fragile autonomy; but sacrifice can also be seen as a devious way of buttressing the self by diminishing it, as Max Horkheimer and Theodor Adorno argue in *Dialectic of Enlightenment*.[13] Humanity, they argue, can exercise dominion over the world all the more effectively by violently laying waste to its own inner nature. Horkheimer and Adorno view ritual sacrifice as among other things a duplicitous ploy to wheedle and hoodwink the Olympians. It may also serve as a way of propitiating Nature for that treasonable abandonment of it which is the precondition of human subjectivity. In his *Lectures on Hegel*, Alexandre Kojève reads the philosopher as arguing that the human subject will sacrifice all, risk everything, stake its very life, for the *summum bonum* of recognition.[14] Indeed, for Hegel subjectivity is itself a form of sacrifice, since to accede to meaning is to abandon being – or as Jacques Lacan puts it, the symbol is the death of the thing. Once reality is articulated, carved up into a play of difference, we shall never recapture that sensuous repleteness we enjoyed before the birth of the signifier, or at least fantasised that we did. At the same time, Hegel refuses throughout his work to regard sacrifice in terms of expiation, seeing it instead as an act of love and gratitude.

In his *Nuer Religion*, E.E. Evans-Pritchard speaks of sacrifice in terms of purchase, indemnification, homage, gift, abnegation, expulsion, ransom, elimination, bargain, exchange, communion, absolution and rebirth. It seems improbable that these wildly diverse functions can be gathered into a single theory.[15] Kathryn McClymond reminds us that death is by no means indispensable to the ceremony: sacrificial tributes can be liquid and vegetal as well as animal.[16] In the Book of Genesis, Cain plumps for the former while Abel opts for the latter. Roger Beckwith points out that the idea of sacrifice in the Christian Gospel spans a number of activities (praise, thanksgiving, prayer, witness, peacemaking, dedication to God and the like) that we ourselves would not customarily include under that heading.[17] For the Hebrew Scriptures, even reading the Torah can be a sacrificial act.

Tylor, as we have seen, is convinced that sacrifice is above all a question of offering gifts to celestial beings. To begin with, he maintains, the gods are thought to appreciate these offerings for what they are in themselves; then they come to be grasped in symbolic terms, as acts of homage and piety; and finally their value is seen to lie in the donor's self-denial. The focus thus shifts from gifts to givers – from gratifying the gods to the spiritual state of those engaged in doing so. William Robertson Smith, by contrast, regards sacrifice as a form of communal feasting, one which powerfully cements social bonds. Marcel Detienne and Jean-Pierre Vernant argue a similar case in *The Cuisine of Sacrifice among the Greeks*. In *The Golden Bough*, James George Frazer prefers to highlight the death of the priest or king. In their classic work *Sacrifice: Its Nature and Functions*, Henri Hubert and Marcel Mauss regard sacrifice primarily as a mediation between sacred and profane domains.

Sacrificial tributes are as diverse as the institution itself. Like the Freudian drive, the impulse to sacrifice would seem (in the phenomenological sense of the term) non-intentional, indifferent to the nature of its object. Edmund Leach points out that for sacrificial purposes the Nuer sometimes replace oxen with wild cucumber.[18] A sheep may be as good as a man for winning divine favour. To speak of such metaphorical substitution is to remind ourselves that there is a semiotics of sacrifice, in which the gift as communicative sign may be purely arbitrary or unmotivated, or where the relation between signifier and signified, donor and offering, is iconic, as when the spotlessness of the gift is taken to signify the blamelessness of the giver. There are also tributes which, like the poetic sign, may be especially communicative precisely because they are rich in inherent value. A donation may be metonymic, in the sense of standing in for the rest of one's material resources, or metaphorical, as with the substitution of beasts for humans. There is a view that a conflict over the semiotics of sacrifice lay behind the fracas unleashed by Jesus over the money changers in the Temple, a brawl that may well have led directly to his execution.[19]

The most compelling version of sacrifice concerns the flourishing of the self, not its extinction. It involves a formidable release of energy, a transformation of the human subject and a turbulent transitus from death to new life.[20] If sacrifice is a political act, it is not least because it concerns an accession to power. As one commentator remarks, 'almost all sacrifice is about power, or powers'.[21] The ritual is indeed about loss and waste, but in the name of a more fruitful form of life. Julian of Norwich sees it in terms of childbirth, where pain is a prelude to joy. If sacrifice involves yielding something up, it is in order to possess it more deeply. As Hubert and Mauss observe, 'there is no sacrifice into which some idea of redemption does not enter'.[22] It is true that the institution has a number of retrograde features, as its critics have been at pains to point out. As we shall see, it has been for the most part a profoundly conservative practice. Yet there is a radical kernel to be extracted from its mystical shell. Sacrifice concerns the passage of the lowly, unremarkable thing from weakness to power. It marks a movement from victimhood to full humanity, destitution to riches, the world as we know it to some transfigured domain. It is this disruptive rite of passage that is known among other things as consecration. To make an object sacred is to mark it out by investing it with a sublimely dangerous power. If sacrifice is often violent, it is because the depth of the change it promises cannot be a matter of smooth evolution or simple continuity.

In this sense, the practice of ritual sacrifice nurtures a wisdom beyond the rationality of the modern, at least at its most callow. It sets its face against the consoling illusion that fulfilment can be achieved without a fundamental rupture and rebirth. The consecration of the sacrificial victim is a matter of wholesale transformation, not some piecemeal evolution. One cannot pass from time to eternity while remaining intact. Since the gods are totally other to humanity, any contact with them involves a metamorphosis as fundamental as the passage from living to dying.[23] The idea of sacrifice broods among other things on the mystery by which life springs from death, seeking a passage through loss and devastation in order to thrive. Dennis J. Schmidt writes of how for Hegel, 'conflict, contradiction, negation,

8

sacrifice, and death saturate the life of the spirit so thoroughly that they define the very truth of the spirit'.[24] In a similar vein, Miguel de Beistegui observes that 'one should recognise that [for Hegel] the greatness of Spirit in history or of man in his action reveals itself primarily in sundering and in death, in sacrifice and in struggle, and that thought itself derives its depth only from taking the full measure of this tragic grandeur'.[25] Pre-modern societies are conscious in a similar way of a secret complicity between living and dying. If the fumes of burnt offerings no longer waft to the nostrils of petulant deities in our own time, it is partly because modernity enforces a rigorous distinction between the two states.

In one ancient view, social existence itself can be sustained only by a power that has passed through death and self-dispossession – through the madness and delirium that Hegel calls the 'Night of the World'. Bridges stay up and crops are persuaded to grow only on account of the consecrated carcasses buried beneath them. Without a cement of innocent blood, writes W.H. Auden in *Horae Canonicae*, no secular wall will ever safely stand. The power of death is pressed into the service of the living, as *thanatos* for Freud conspires with *eros* to pluck a civilisation from the mire. In this sense, it is death that brings the value of life into focus. 'In the experience of killing', writes Walter Burkert in a comment on sacrifice, 'one perceives the sacredness of life; it is nourished and perpetuated by death.'[26] In tribal societies, he adds, the power to kill and a respect for life are mutually illuminating. The modern practice of suicide is a monstrous perversion of the belief that life springs from self-dispossession.

'In its most extreme form', comments George Heyman, 'the act of sacrificial killing affirms and enhances life itself.'[27] Ritual sacrifice is affirmative in a number of ways: because the slaughtered victim enters by its death upon eternal life, becoming all-powerful and invulnerable in the process; because its loss makes us freshly conscious of the fragility of life, which in turn enriches our sense of its preciousness; and because to destroy the offering serves by contrast to highlight the boundless reserves of natural and human existence, which can easily survive such a privation. The slaying of the sacrificial tribute signifies a radical self-dispossession on the part of the donor, which is in turn made possible by an exuberant excess of life. Only one furnished with such prodigious riches, such as Friedrich Nietzsche's Übermensch, would feel self-assured enough to yield up a portion of them. The Übermensch sacrifices others for the greater good of the species, but he also makes sacrifices himself, bestowing his largesse upon those around him. 'It is richness in personality, abundance in oneself', Nietzsche writes in *The Will to Power*, 'overflowing and bestowing, instinctive good health and affirmation of oneself, that produce great sacrifice and great love.'[28] Yet if giving is as easy as this, a spontaneous overflow from one's ceaselessly replenished depths, it is hard to see how one can speak of it as sacrifice at all, any more than one can speak of Timon's reckless self-squandering in Shakespeare's *Timon of Athens* as a form of self-abandonment. If the self's powers are fathomless, there can be no question of dispossession.

'Whatever is to endure and be effective', writes Burkert, 'must pass through a sacrifice which opens the abyss of annihilation.'[29] 'The life of the Spirit', Hegel writes in a legendary sentence in *Phenomenology of Spirit*, 'is not the life that shrinks from death and keeps itself untouched by devastation, but rather the life that endures it and maintains itself within it.'[30] He speaks of 'the tragedy which the Absolute eternally enacts with itself, by eternally giving birth to itself into objectivity, submitting in this objective form to passion and death, and rising from its ashes in glory.'[31] The Hegelian Absolute is thus sacrificial in its inmost structure, losing itself in otherness and negativity as a prelude to reuniting with itself, descending into hell in order to be reborn as affirmative Spirit. Finitude must negate itself in order to come into its own. The Absolute must renounce itself in entering upon material existence, rather as Christ represents the Father's kenotic self-abandonment. In the act of sacrifice, the absolute nature of death invests those mortal things that can expose themselves to its terror with an imperishable form of life. For Christian faith, only an existence tempered and refined by death, having passed through the symbolic drowning of baptism and fed in sign on the flesh of a martyr, is resilient enough to overcome sin (rape, genocide, slavery, exploitation and the like). If some cultures know this transitus as sacrifice, others give it the name of tragedy. There are also places (ancient Greece, for example) where this obscure affinity between living and dying goes under both titles.[32]

'In modernity', writes Giorgio Agamben, 'the principle of the sacredness of life is ... completely emancipated from sacrificial ideology.'[33] For this ideology, there is an obscene underside to everyday existence, a tell-tale bloodstain imprinted on its fabric, with which its ceremonial rites seek to come to terms. Nietzsche saw sacrifice in the sense of an inescapable cruelty and exploitation lying at the foundation of human culture, and so as a phenomenon to be celebrated. In the words of one commentator, sacrifice is aware of 'a brokenness at the basis and origin of life'.[34] It can signify a return to the origins of the tribe or nation, and as such involves a meditation on the violence of that inaugural moment, one which continues to undergird social existence. The springing of life from death is, among other things, the emergence of civilisation from barbarism. Most civilised orders are the fruit of carnage, dispossession, occupation, usurpation or extermination. There is little the founders of nations need to be told about original sin. As Marcel Detienne writes, 'The fatherland, property, work, the human person, are all to be credited to sacrifice as a social phenomenon.'[35] Hegel sees history as a slaughter bench on which innumerable sacrifices have been performed. However deeply these primordial trespasses are thrust into the political unconscious, the guilt they breed continues to fester, and it is not hard to see sacrifice as one means of seeking to assuage it, as well as being part of the violence and brutality to which it offers a symbolic solution. The Real or blood offering which lies at the root of the symbolic order is unable to figure fully within it; but like a banished ghost lurking at its edges, it can be evoked in the act of sacrifice by a symbolic performance, glimpsed in stylised form, shown rather than stated. In reliving this primordial act of violence, men and women acknowledge themselves to be dependent on certain capricious, sublimely impenetrable powers which they are unable to bend to their own purposes without danger of hubris and impiety. In this sense, sacrifice is a critique of the ethic of self-sovereignty. It recognises the self as an effect of the Other. One's identity is not one's own, but lies in the keeping of the gods.[36]

Like repression in the judgement of Freud, sacrifice is doomed to be a recurrent process rather than a punctual event. If its gestures of homage and reparation must be endlessly repeated, it is among other things because the violence that sustains the social order cannot be fully dredged to consciousness. It is on such collective amnesia that civilisation thrives. As long as society continues to breed conflict and repression, it remains caught within the ambit of its bloody origins, unable to break out of that long catastrophe into history proper. Instead, the human narrative becomes a series of ingeniously innovative ways of disavowing its own disreputable parentage. If we desire a future, it is partly in order to bury the past.

It is possible to see sacrifice as involving an exchange of powers. There is that which must be lost for the sake of a greater gain. Rather as the gods grant you a military victory in return for an appropriate number of mutilated oxen, so in Freud's eyes civilisation itself turns upon a sacrificial compact. In a *felix culpa* or fortunate Fall, we pay for our cathedrals and civic institutions in the coinage of repression and neurosis, accepting a certain loss of *jouissance* or shedding of a symbolic pound of flesh in return for our accession to language, identity and the symbolic order. The human subject who sacrifices this or that gratifying object is able to do so only because of a deeper trade-off or primordial act of forfeiture, one which is constitutive of subjectivity itself. At the root of human history lies a self-dispossession so deep-seated that any complete recovery from it is out of the question. If it is the gods who help to foster guilt in pre-modern cultures, in Freud's view it is the Law of the Father or superego that represents a pure culture of the death drive in modern times. As in the rite of sacrifice, guilt, death, compulsive repetition, symbolic displacement, the suspension of time, the need to expiate some nameless guilt and the urge to self-extinction converge in a single lethal syndrome. Ritual

13

sacrifice, like neurosis, is a sign of the problem to which it offers a dubious solution. Only by overthrowing the punitive Law of the Father could this whole deadly dispensation be set aside. We shall see later that this is part of the significance of Calvary.

* * *

Let us turn briefly to a literary example of the relations between violence and civilisation. The founding of a civilisation is the *telos* of Virgil's *Aeneid*, but it is an endpoint beset with troubles. The gods scrap among themselves, prophecies may be dark and uncertain, and hubris may erupt to wreck the best-laid providential schemes. Rather as for Freud, *eros* finds its path to its true home (death) only by the series of digressions and diversions known as life, so Aeneas, homesick for a future that he will not live to see, is delayed by various plot entanglements which impede his historic mission. He must extricate himself from these distractions, leaving the grief-stricken Dido behind and resisting the lure of premature settlements (Thrace, Crete, Carthage, Sicily). *Eros* may be the driving force of the civilising process, but in the form of love imbroglios it can also fatally obstruct it. The poem presents erotic love as a question of violence, madness, poison, wounding, fatality and deadly affliction, so that desire must be deferred, the reality principle allowed to triumph over the pleasure principle, if the coherent thrust of the narrative is not to disintegrate into so many fragmentary episodes. As the bearer of a lineage, a divine destiny or historic project, Aeneas is no more a free agent than any other literary character, and must forgo his gratification if civilisation is to be established. At the same time, the various detours and deviations from that end are what constitute the story. The goddess Juno is powerless to thwart the Trojans' final arrival in Latium, but she can delay that triumph by fomenting war, and without such deferments there would be no narrative.

In Freud's view, *eros* finds its beginning in its end, as the ego discovers in death a refuge akin to the blissful state that reigned before it embarked on its ill-starred journey. Dido discovers her own version of such a sanctuary in the act of suicide. The erotic as regressive pleasure thus has a tendency to elide the business of narrative, curving back constantly to an earlier state of affairs and thus posing a threat to *eros* as builder of cities and historical project. Yet that, too, is a matter of regress as well as progress. The Rome that Aeneas is seeking to establish is likewise a return to origins, since the Trojan nation itself was founded by the Italian warrior Dardanus. As a second Troy, Rome is the repetition of an origin, eliding time in the manner of *eros*. Prophecy, too, garbles time, folding the future into the present. As its name suggests, Latium is a place of hiding, a region in which Saturn, fleeing from Jupiter, sought shelter; and it is here that the bruised and battered voyagers will finally come to rest, as the bruised and battered ego in Freud's view will ultimately find its resting place.

So it is that Virgil's great epic records the violent pre-history of the Roman nation, forging a shapely narrative from the tumult of war and the chaos of Nature rather as civilisation itself plucks a coherent project from these unruly forces. Rome has its murky roots in the rapine and atrocity of the Trojan war, and the city's remote progenitor, Aeneas, is an outcast and wanderer, leader of a rootless, buffeted, war-weary remnant who form a fragile link between past and present. Yet this history of senseless warfare and spiteful deities is converted by the poem itself into a prolegomenon to the glorious present. Otherwise random episodes are stitched into the seamless continuity of Providence, alchemised into the sacred provenance of the nation. We know that Aeneas will achieve his goal because the poem itself exists in all its burnished splendour, the fruit of a nation that can now glance over its shoulder and survey its own barbarous beginnings, assured that this history of carnage has issued in a felicitous end. Rome now exerts dominion over the various powers that sought to wreck the process of its emergence, powers of which Aeneas and his companions are often enough portrayed as the helpless playthings. The narrative of national destiny has triumphed over a pre-history of misfortune.

Once it is established, however, civilisation by no means provides respite from the bloodstained narrative that went into its making. On the contrary, it is largely a perpetuation of that grim tale – a higher form of barbarism, so to speak, under the name of law, empire and universal order. Civilised society, with its endless imperial expansion, proves to be the reverse of a resting place, as Rome visits on less well-favoured peoples the mayhem and carnage from which it itself arose, thus returning to its own origins in a rather less glorious sense than the production of national monuments like the *Aeneid*. The violence which was the prelude to civility continues to flourish within that civilised condition, mitigated in some ways by its doctrines and technologies yet in other ways intensified by them. Among other things, those anarchic forces are sublimated into the legitimate violence of the law, which helps to secure the conditions within which national epics like the *Aeneid* can be written. As Slavoj Žižek remarks, such law represents 'the violence which sustains the very containment of violence'.[37] In the licensed aggression of the judiciary and armed forces, barbarism and civilisation are now well-nigh indistinguishable. The final guarantee of civility is state-sanctioned death.[38] Yet this state of affairs had long been anticipated. In myth, writes Walter Burkert, 'the most gruesome tales of living creatures torn apart and of cannibalism are presented in conjunction with the achievements of civilised life'.[39] In the ambivalences of myth, as well as in that coupling of the blessed and the cursed known as the sacred, one can glimpse a recognition that death and dismemberment lurk at the source of peace and prosperity.

In Aeschylus's *Oresteia*, the fearful forces that rage beyond the pale of civilisation and threaten to thrust it back into primeval slime will finally be enshrined within its borders, as the Furies are metamorphosed into the Eumenides or Kindly Ones. Figures of terror in pre-modern times must be sweet-talked and cajoled, treated in a diplomatic fiction as good-hearted and well disposed, which is one reason for the blurring of boundaries between the horrific and the holy signified by the word 'sacred'. That which threatens to sink social order without trace is appropriated, sublimated and turned outwards, converted into a defence against the city's foes. In an arresting paradox, the violence which salvaged civilisation from dust and slime now takes the form of the law that protects it from both outside invasion and internal insurrection. Barbarism and civilisation are synchronous rather than sequential, two sides of the same coin rather than consecutive historical stages. One must acknowledge that there are forces constitutive of human culture that are also capable of tearing it apart.

Sacrifice is among other things a way of seeking to accommodate these death-dealing yet potentially world-creating powers, clinging to the claims of civility while recognising their dependence on divine or demonic energies which run deeper than rationality. If reason is to flourish, it must be conscious of its own modest capabilities, illuminating those shadowy frontiers where it trails off into darkness and non-being. What is true of the *Oresteia* in this respect is also the case in Euripides' *The Bacchae*. The self must be founded on the non-self, law and order on pain and terror, the polis on a refined version of the very savagery it has apparently put behind it. You must seek to win over these sacred powers through an act of symbolic identification with them, but not to the point where, like Pentheus in *The Bacchae*, they end up tearing you limb from limb. To greet them with due reverence is not to capitulate to them. Instead, they must be incorporated into the social order, not least in the form of the sublime terror of the Law, so that consent to political authority may be reinforced with coercion. The problem is how such coercion is to buttress consent rather than destroy it. There is no sacrifice without a seething undercurrent of *ressentiment*, no meek obeisance to the governing powers that does not harbour a smouldering animus against them. Since a being who confers his favour upon you demonstrates his superiority by doing so, your gratitude for his largesse is bound to be laced with a certain disgruntlement. It is partly to assuage the guilt of this animosity that we must repair to the altar once more, in search of that pure, unspotted self-abnegation before the Law that lies perpetually beyond our reach.

* * *

It would be possible to recount a narrative of how the ritual slaughter of human beings (in so far as such a custom ever thrived) gives way

18

to tributes of grain or goats, and how in modern times this is in turn subject to a further displacement, as the act of sacrifice becomes both introverted and sublimated. It is now recast as an internal victory over one's turbulent desires, a question of self-discipline and self-repression. Sacrifice is the shadow cast by the urge to self-sovereignty of the modern age. 'Well it is, not only for the priest but for mankind', observes James George Frazer, 'when with the slow progress of civilisation and humanity the hard facts of a cruel ritual have thus been softened and diluted with the nebulous abstractions of a mystical theology.'[40] Frazer has little time for either sacrificial rites or mystical theology; but the latter, which sublimates the violence of the former into the self-government of the docile citizen, at least represents an advance on so-called ritual homicide.

The history of civilisation, write Horkheimer and Adorno in *Dialectic of Enlightenment*, is the history of the introversion of sacrifice.[41] Max Weber thought that the idea of progress had rendered the notion of death meaningless, reducing it to a mere transition to the eternal life of the future. I die, but the species lives on, and flourishes all the more vigorously the more it evolves. Even so, one might claim that for humanity to move forward, it must immolate both past and present on the altar of the future. *Dialectic of Enlightenment* sees the very structure of the ego as sacrificial, deferring gratification so that history might be born. Only by abjuring the self can one secure the social order which would allow it to thrive. In this sense, from Rousseau and Kant to Comte and Freud, sacrifice lies as much at the foundation of the modern social order as it does of the ancient.

There are others for whom art, not society, is the altar on which the ego is to be sacrificially slain. From Flaubert to Joyce, the artist becomes a secular priest, transubstantiating the profane materials of everyday life into something rich and rare. Since he immolates his own existence for the sake of his art, he is priest and victim in one body, and is in this sense akin to the martyr. Like Christ, he descends into the foul rag and bone shop of the heart, the cesspit of human squalor and despair, in order to gather it into the artifice of eternity, transmuting its unsavoury materials into works of imperishable glory. The imagination is a form of self-dispossession, seizing selflessly on its object; yet it is by means of this constant surging beyond itself that the self is enriched.

In the course of time, then, the idea of sacrifice shifts from the business of ritual slaughter to a question of moral conduct. Yet these two versions of the concept are already at loggerheads with each other in the Hebrew Scriptures. There is some debate over how favourably those writings look upon ritual sacrifice. Certainly there is a powerful prophetic tradition denouncing it. 'I desire loving kindness, not sacrifice, the knowledge of God rather than burnt offerings', Hosea has Yahweh declare (Hosea 6:6). The God of the Book of Amos tells the Israelites that he despises their sacrificial feasts and spurns their burnt offerings. Instead, he calls for justice to flow down like water. In Jeremiah, God reminds his pathologically idolatrous people that he has commanded nothing about sacrificial offerings.[42] Isaiah's exasperated deity informs the Jews that he is sick of their burnt offerings and nauseated by the smoke which wafts to heaven from them. They should be protecting the poor from the violence of the rich, not practising these empty rites of propitiation. The hands of those making sacrifice, Isaiah protests, are covered with blood, meaning that those who bloody their hands for sacred ends have stained them already with impious ones. Max Weber speaks accordingly of an 'ethical turn' in the Hebrew Scriptures, at odds with all 'known mythologies of the dying and resurrected vegetation gods or other deities and heroes'.[43]

There is abundant evidence that the God of the Jewish Bible takes no delight in the cultic slaughter of beasts, and is impervious to the blandishments with which these carcasses are thrust upon his attention. He cannot be inveigled by such overtures because he is a non-god, a god of the poor rather than of burnt offerings, but also because he is inconceivably other, which is one reason why Islam, too, rejects the possibility of a symbolic or sacrificial exchange with Allah. In any case, such ritual demonstrations of piety will never succeed in propitiating the savage powers that undergird the social order, which is why they must be compulsively repeated. An endless metonymic succession of burnt offerings and slaughtered beasts must seek to appease gods who are immune to such haggling, as well as to atone for a guilt in which we take a secret relish. The more obdurate the deities appear, contemptuously spurning our paltry tributes, the more guilt and uncertainty we accumulate, which then impels us to the altar once again, and so on in a bad infinity of botched reparations. The gods demand sacrifice; but this is something of a sick joke, since they are as conscious of the fact that we cannot placate them as the superego is sadistically aware that the ego can never match up to its pitiless diktats. Rather as the Lacanian subject can never be certain whether it has been recognised by the Other, so the gods' response to our cajolery is sibylline and elusive. The *deus absconditus* of radical Protestantism is an alarmingly inscrutable figure, as impossible to please as a capricious rock

21

star or peevish prima donna. Sacrifice will come to an end only when the lowly represented by its offerings come to power in reality. There will be no religious cult in the New Jerusalem. We can never be justified before the Law, whose fury and vindictiveness are simply stoked by our self-prostration. Even so, in soft-soaping the gods into gratifying your desire, you score an agreeable victory over them, bending them to your will while obsequiously bowing the knee.

Yahweh is not in general presented by the Scriptures as a wrathful deity who needs to be kept sweet. A god who loves his creatures so dearly that he is prepared to be done to death by them clearly requires no appeasing. The notion of sacrifice as mutually profitable exchange – of *do ut des*, or giving in order to get back – is untypical of the Hebrew Bible. If sacrifice is indeed acceptable to the Old Testament, it is as a matter of love, praise, repentance, thanksgiving and the like, not as a species of divine lobbying. That this is so is worth underlining. Ancient peoples did not typically perform sacrifice out of affection for their divine superiors, or imagine that the gods were besotted with them. It was a far more prudential affair. It is not religious cult, then, that gladdens Yahweh's heart. 'Burnt offerings and sin offerings thou hast not required', claims Psalm 40. Jesus insists in Mark's Gospel that to love God amounts to more than all sacrifices and burnt offerings. Even as capacious a document as Second Isaiah alludes to sacrifice only on a single occasion. The Letter to the Hebrews warns that 'it is not possible that the blood of bulls and goats can take away sin' (Hebrews 10:4). For this epistle, Christ's redemption of humanity has brought the institution of sacrifice to a definitive conclusion. The whole cultic business – what Walter Benjamin calls in his essay on 'Fate and Character' the endless pagan chain of guilt and atonement – is now washed up, *dépassé*, dead and done with. This is one death that will not need to be compulsively recycled. The author of Hebrews points out with refreshing bluntness that if ritual sacrifice were really successful, it would have ceased already, having accomplished its aim.[44] Like capital punishment, its persistence simply points up its ineffectiveness. 'The repetition of sacrifice', writes C.F.D. Moule, 'is its own indictment.'[45] All ritual sacrifice ends in failure, and thus has to be ceaselessly repeated, not least because it seeks to placate indifferent or vindictive deities who are frostily immune to being beguiled.

In a magisterial study, Robert J. Daly notes an ambiguity on the question of ritual sacrifice in the New Testament. Jesus reveals some positive or at least neutral attitudes to the practice, but he is never once shown engaging in it. On the other hand, if he really did repudiate sacrifice, then as Paula Fredriksen points out, he would have been utterly unique among the Jews and even Gentiles of his time.[46] Mark's Jesus is somewhat hostile to traditional Judaic observances, whereas Matthew's is not. Gospel evidence against the relevance of ritual sacrifice is not hard to come by. 'A more startling claim could hardly have been made' is Daly's verdict on Jesus's grossly provocative pulling of rank over the revered site of such practices, the Jewish Temple ('I tell you, something greater than the Temple is here').[47] In Paul's First Letter to the Corinthians, it is the human body and the Christian community which constitute the new Temple. The sacred arena is now a phenomenological space constituted by the presence of human bodies to one other, not a topographical terrain. And this liturgical space is both mobile and potentially universal, as the Temple was not. In the Acts of the Apostles, Paul and Barnabas condemn animal sacrifice as entirely useless. The Gospel holds up a Samaritan as morally exemplary, though the Samaritans were by no means admirers of Jewish sacrificial cult. One can interpret the New Testament as holding that Jesus replaces ritual sacrifice with love and service. St John speaks of sacrifice in moral rather than cultic terms. It is a matter of laying down one's life for others, and thus an ethico-political affair, not primarily a question of religious observance. If ritual sacrifice does indeed make sense, it is only within such a context. There are similar protests against the custom in ancient Greece. Empedocles and Theophrastus both condemn it. Varro denies that the gods demand blood, while Seneca insists that the essence of sacrifice lies not in slaughtered beasts but in the righteous disposition of those who worship the Olympians. Lucian of Samosata holds that anyone who observes sacrificial rituals can only laugh at their stupidity.[48]

It was the exile of the Israelites and the destruction of the Temple that forced the moral or spiritual aspects of sacrifice to the fore, given that, with the loss of the appropriate space for its performance, the cultic version of the practice was brought to an end. It was now to be virtualised and internalised, kept alive in the hearts and minds of the people like a lost leader or half-obliterated origin. As Michael Fishbane puts it, 'the end of sacrifices has to be dealt with, and to fill the breach rabbinic Judaism had to reach into its innermost and most authentic (ethical) resources'.[49] Shorn of its ritual context, the spiritual significance of the act could more easily be retrieved. Acts of love and mercy come to assume pride of place over donations of corn or the shedding of lambs' blood. It is the lowly of spirit who are great in God's esteem, not goats or handfuls of grain. Arrogance and stiff-necked pride must be yielded up in place of beasts. A quasi-magical view of sacrifice, for which atonement is achieved *ex opere operato* by the mere execution of the rite, must yield ground to a moral consciousness for which burnt offerings are valid only as signifiers of contrition and humility. Perhaps it was against this reifying of the practice, rather than against the institution as such, that the prophets launched their polemic. The oblation that counts is the surrender of one's selfish interests for the sake of others. 'Prayers and giving of thanks', writes Justin Martyr, '. . . are the only perfect and well-pleasing sacrifices to God.'[50] Sacrifice becomes self-sacrifice. For the Augustine of *De Civitate Dei*, the kernel of the custom is love and mercy. At the same time, the people of a building become the people of a book. The loss of the Temple means that God's presence is to be found in scripture rather than material space. Since writing, like Yahweh, transcends locality and avoids being nailed down to a rigidly determinate meaning, the substitution is an appropriate one.

Even so, most commentators doubt that the cultic and ethical meanings of sacrifice in the New Testament are fundamentally in conflict.[51] Psalm 51 declares that Yahweh has no desire for a sacrificial cult since 'the sacrifice acceptable to God is a broken spirit; a broken and contrite heart, O God, thou wilt not despise'. Yet the same text also calls for 'right sacrifices, in burnt offerings and whole burnt offerings', with no apparent sense of inconsistency. The two meanings converge in the Crucifixion, which dramatically seals the relation between physical sacrifice and spiritual self-dispossession. Besides, even the sternest critics of ritual sacrifice saw the suspension of the institution with the loss of the Temple as purely temporary.

The narrative that the New Testament has to recount is not a tale of how history has progressed in civilised spirit from sacrifice as homicide to some more gentrified version of the practice, but exactly the reverse. It is the tale of how sacrifice as selfless devotion is likely to result in a bloody execution at the hands of the state. (Denys Turner speaks of Jesus being 'extra-judicially executed on the majority recommendation of a corrupt committee of very religious people'.)[52] Such are the powers of this world, as St John terms the sovereign political regimes, that a loyalty to the dispossessed of the kind Jesus demonstrates is likely to confront the ruling class with a threat to its stability. A devotion to the dispossessed is a familiar prelude to a bloody death at the hands of the political state. So it is that the violence of carving up bullocks gives way to the firepower of the political establishment. As one commentator remarks, the violence of the cross 'is not divine violence at all but rather human violence dissembled by means of the sacred into the will of the idolised gods'.[53] What is revolutionary about the death of Jesus is not primarily that it unmasks the institution of sacrifice as barbaric, as René Girard argues, but that it lays bare the barbarism of the ruling powers. The purity of the victim is no longer that of doves or calves, who are innocent only in the sense that moral concepts have no bearing on them, but is that of the blameless just, on whose heads a virulent political aggression is unleashed. What is now at stake is not a placating of the gods but political murder. It is as though the saga of sacrifice is looped upon itself, beginning (so it is supposed) with the slaughter of human beings, moving on to certain symbolic surrogates for them, next shifting up a gear, so to speak, to the ethical realm, and then, when this is pressed to an extreme, turning once more on a mutilated body.

In a strange dialectical turn, then, one of the most savage of human actions (human sacrifice) reappears in the guise of martyrdom as one of the most sublimely ethical ones.[54] Calvary is a scene of carnage, like the bloodstained sacrificial altar, but it is also a site of supreme value. In this incongruous coupling of features, it is curiously akin to tragic theatre. It is Jesus's dedication to justice and fellowship that delivers him to the cross. His solidarity with those who dwell in the borderlands of orthodox society, men and women whose existence signifies a kind of non-being, prefigures the non-being to which he himself is brought on the outer edge of the metropolis. In the person of Jesus, those whom Paul calls the filth of the earth are in principle raised up to glory. So it is that an act of state brutality also signifies a symbolic undoing of political violence. Power is now, in principle, in the hands of those whom it has traditionally spurned as so much refuse and garbage. If the founding act of civilisation involves a gesture of exclusion, this new regime reverses that repression, as the slab rejected by the builders becomes the cornerstone of a new dispensation.

It is in this sense that Jesus, as Agamben comments of *homo sacer*, 'preserves the meaning of the original exclusion through which the political dimension was first constituted.'[55] It is divine law which is now subversive, as the claims of justice confront the insolence of authority. What is transgressive is the comradeship Jesus preaches. Authentic power is at war with the status quo, given that its source lies in a solidarity with weakness. In the 'victorious defeat' of his death, to steal a phrase from Nietzsche, Jesus lives out as free decision the destitution into which others are forced by dire circumstance. The only enduring power is one salvaged from frailty, which as Saul Bellow's Moses Herzog ruefully observes, is not the opinion of this world: 'This generation thinks ... that nothing faithful,

vulnerable, fragile, can be durable or have any true power'. As John
Milbank comments, 'if we are all terminally fragile, then our temporary lives assume an ultimate value, since we can offer our own lives
for the sake of others'.[56]

What is at stake on Calvary is an *Aufhebung* of sacrifice rather
than a simple negation of it. The practice is both consummated and
annulled. Jean-Luc Nancy speaks of Christianity as involving 'the
sacrifice of sacrifice'.[57] The cross stands in an ancient tradition of
sacrifice while also spelling its demise. If it consigns ritual slaughter
to the benighted past, it is itself a matter of bloodshed and barbarism.
For D.R. Jones, 'sacrifice is pre-eminently bloody sacrifice', despite
what he sees as the gradual spiritualising of the custom to be
found in so many religious traditions.[58] The Letter to the Hebrews,
in the words of one scholar, 'affirms and transforms the sacrificial
system while working within it'.[59] As such, it represents in the
strict sense of the term a deconstruction, occupying the logic of
sacrifice from within in order to expose its fatal flaws. Hebrews
sees Jesus as having entered into the forbidden precinct of the
Temple, a place reserved for the priestly caste, and in doing so
dismantling from within that hallowed enclave the very distinction
between sacred and secular, thus consigning the protocols of this
venerable site to the ashcan of history. A bloody political murder
now occupies the place of the Holy of Holies. Sacred times and
places are now at an end, since martyrdom can happen anywhere;
and all those who can recognise themselves in this bloody business
are potential martyrs, baptised into Jesus's death. They must make
this abject failure their own. Only through such mimesis can they
achieve authenticity.

Having entered the Holy of Holies, Jesus will offer up not animals but himself, replacing the Temple (meaning the entire apparatus of priestly and political power) with his own flesh and blood, and in doing so bringing ritual sacrifice to a finish. There is an endless supply of calves and bullocks to be laid on the altar, but once one has rejected this metonymy or symbolic substitutionism and offered one's own life instead, one cannot do so again.[60] Jesus's crucifixion and resurrection constitute in Alain Badiou's term an 'event', a revolutionary transformation which breaks with the sterile pre-history of ritual sacrifice and inaugurates a future in which there will be no temple or religious cult.[61] For Badiou, events of this kind are utterly original, quasi-miraculous occurrences founded purely in themselves, moments of pure rupture or primordial beginnings which are out of joint with their historical 'sites', in excess of their contexts, sprung (as it were) *ex nihilo* from empirical situations that could not have pre-calculated them. It is thus that the Resurrection breaks into the disciples' defeatist gloom after Calvary with all the illogicality of a Dadaist happening, inaugurating the unimaginably avant-garde reality of the kingdom of God. Yet this new creation is made possible only by Jesus's passage through the very sacrificial institution that has now been definitively surpassed.

Chapter 2

TRAGEDY AND CRUCIFIXION

WALTER BENJAMIN'S THEORY of tragedy in his *The Origin of German Tragic Drama* has some affinities with the Christian view of Calvary. Tragedy for Benjamin is essentially sacrifice, but of a peculiarly doubled kind: if it propitiates the gods under ancient law, it also inaugurates a revolutionary new order which promises to undermine that dispensation. As Simon Sparks writes, 'An expiatory sacrifice according to the letter of the ancient law, tragic death also tears the pages from that book in the spirit of the laws of the new community, consigning them – along with the hero – to ashes in the rites of the funeral pyre.'[1] Tragedy for Benjamin is both archaic and avant-garde, as is so much of the modernism with which he is associated. It represents a hinge or transition between two epochs, shifting as it does from fate to freedom, myth to truth, pagan ritual to the ethico-political, the oppressive order of the gods to that of a redeemed people; and the death of the protagonist marks the turbulent passing over from the one to the other.

Calvary fulfils almost none of the conditions for the appropriate performance of sacrificial rites, which is why to call it a sacrifice at all is to transform the very concept. For one thing, human oblations were not of course acceptable to the Jews. For another thing, the event does not take place in the Temple, and there is no priest to conduct the ceremony. Jesus was not a member of the sacerdotal caste but an obscure layman, a blow-in from provincial Galilee, probably the son of a stonemason. The offering itself is blemished beyond repair, cursed by crucifixion. Jesus is *ungeheuer*, *homo sacer*, an outcast animal or contaminated creature with no ordained place in the cosmic or symbolic order. To insist on calling the event a sacrifice, however, even though it is plainly not, is to extract something of the true significance of the practice from the myths in which it is enmeshed. It is a sacrificial act because it concerns the passage of a humble, victimised thing from weakness to power.[2] One cannot pass from time to eternity while remaining intact. To slay a thing sacrificially is to withdraw it from the domain of human dealings so that it re-emerges precious and pregnant with new meaning in the sphere of the gods. Since these divine beings are wholly other than humanity, any such perilous contact with them brings with it a metamorphosis as thoroughgoing as a conversion from death to life.[3]

If ritual sacrifice is outmoded by Calvary, it is also because the cross represents a kind of *comédie noire* or carnivalesque parody of the practice, one in which the relations between donor and recipient are satirically reframed.[4] It is now God himself who is the flayed, bloodied victim, and one, moreover, who identifies with his executioners by forgiving them, not least on account of their false consciousness. The event is at once an act of murder and an act of pardon, for this and all other crimes. The sheer terror of Yahweh is

31

not effaced but reinterpreted. Yahweh is indeed terrible to look upon, but what is now revealed as sublime about him is his brutally unconditional love, symbolised in the annihilating black lightning of William Golding's novel *Pincher Martin*. For Henri Hubert and Marcel Mauss, sacrifice inserts a protective medium (the sacrificial tribute itself) between humanity and the sublime fury of the gods.[5] In the Crucifixion, by contrast, it is as though the devastating rage of divine love is focused in the body of Jesus, as the power which allows it to pass through humiliation and death to emerge somewhere on the other side.

It is God who is divested of himself in pain and terror, in a caustic critique of the idolatrous image of him as patriarch and potentate. In a daring gesture of self-debunkery, the Messiah himself is pinned to a cross. The notion of a crucified Messiah would have struck the Jews of the time as an unspeakable moral obscenity. The only good god is a dead one. The sardonic sign above Jesus's cross – 'Jesus of Nazareth, King of the Jews' – could be read as a calculated piece of bathos, the equivalent of which today (Nazareth being a provincial backwater) might be 'Fred Smith of Barnsley, President of the Universe'. It is as though the event presses the institution of sacrifice to a surreal extreme, and in doing so dispenses with it altogether. The scandalous, indecorous, darkly comic idea of an all-loving deity being carved up by his own creatures belongs as much to farce as to high tragedy. If it is horrifying, it is also embarrassing. It seems as likely to provoke a fit of hysterical laughter as tears of bitter remorse. There is a touch of grotesquerie in the prospect of a merciful god flying to the rescue of his people only to be done to death by them in a bout of political panic. Calvary is a place of savage bathos as well as a site of torture.

* * *

There is a current of tragic theory for which the hero stoops to conquer, bowing to his destiny but transcending it in that very act. To will the dissolution of the self is at the same time to rise above it, since only the staunchest of wills is capable of disposing of itself so courageously. The highest freedom is to opt for one's own extinction. In resolutely embracing his own destruction, the tragic hero manifests the indomitable spirit of humanity as such, which shines out in all its resplendent glory against the background of his voluntary self-oblation. His death is thus loss and gain in a single gesture. As with the martyr, freedom can be achieved only through its negation, and affirmation only through its denial. The tragic hero is the 'guilty innocent' who embraces his own crime even though, like Oedipus, it was forced upon him by fate, assuming responsibility for all that he has done and making his destiny his own. As such, he mixes defiance and submission in equal measure, fusing rebellion and authority, will and law, spirit and nature. The tragic here is essentially a question of reconciliation.[6] In a striking irony, what it resolves is the supposedly irreconcilable clash of forces known as tragedy.

Moreover, in submitting to his destiny, the hero reveals that this very power is at work within himself, lying as it does at the source of his free decision. There is an inner necessity about the passion for liberty, so that freedom and fate are revealed to be one. Besides, freedom can only become conscious of itself in experiencing the

33

recalcitrance of the world, its stubborn resistance to its projects, so that in this sense, too, liberty and destiny are closely linked. Freedom without resistance would simply implode. In disclosing the grandeur of the protagonist, then, tragedy also glorifies the law to which he voluntarily submits. At the end of Friedrich Schiller's *The Robbers*, the criminal Karl Moor hands himself over to the laws against which he has offended in order 'to make manifest their invulnerable majesty to all mankind'. Moral order is restored by tragic sacrifice. The play thus sends a salutary message in advance to the French revolutionaries. Freedom must be affirmed, but only in a way that conforms to law and order, a paradox of which tragedy is the paradigm. Tragic freedom is the true essence of political liberty.

The spectators of these events are edified as well as chastened. They leave the theatre with a keener sense of the fragility of life, but also with an enhanced sense of its value. To annihilate created things, not least Man himself, is to show them up as fragile and fugitive, and thus by contrast to pay homage to the eternal. In the dismembering of humanity, we are witness to an epiphany of the Absolute. The closest humanity can approach to this sublime condition is to acknowledge its own finitude, an acknowledgement consummated in the decision to die. As Friedrich Schlegel writes,

> The hidden meaning of sacrifice is the annihilation of the finite because it is finite. In order to demonstrate that this is its only justification, one must choose to sacrifice whatever is most noble and most beautiful; but particularly man, the flower of the earth . . . hence man can only sacrifice himself . . . In the enthusiasm of annihilation, the meaning of the divine creation is realised for

the first time. Only in the midst of death does the lightning bolt of eternal life explode.[7]

'What I am after', writes Eugene O'Neill, 'is to get an audience leaving the theatre with an exultant feeling from seeing somebody on the stage facing life, fighting against the eternal odds, not conquering, but perhaps inevitably being conquered. The individual life is made significant just by the struggle.'[8] It is the aesthetic of an age for which defeat is more common than victory, but which nevertheless refuses to relinquish a sense of affirmation. In identifying with the protagonist, the spectators can know the self-lacerating delights of being torn to pieces, transferring their own mortality onto his shoulders; but at the same time they can exult in the sadistic pleasure of surviving him, thus indulging an agreeable fantasy of immortality. Their lives can now feed off his for a while, until a new sacrificial victim happens along. It is thus that tragedy bears witness to the truth that in the midst of death we are in life. Besides, in framing and stylising death, tragic art intimates a passage beyond it. Its very artistic form is a species of theodicy, constituting a symbolic victory over the terrors of its content. Theodor Adorno, by contrast, protests against the use of aesthetic stylisation to find some meaning in human horror. In his view, something is thereby subtracted from that suffering, and the victims are accordingly wronged.[9]

The ideology of tragedy we have just sketched, one to be found also in the work of Schelling and Hölderlin, takes its cue from, among other things, a triumphalist reading of the Crucifixion. It is a view that is in danger of glorifying death, magnifying the will and idealising the tragic hero. It is also at risk of buying its transcendence on the cheap, without reckoning its cost in human hardship. Here, the aesthetic meaning of tragedy drifts free of the everyday sense. Friedrich Nietzsche comes up with a rather more bullish version of this tragic triumphalism. For the authentically tragic vision, 'life itself, its eternal fruitfulness and recurrence, creates torment, destruction, the will to annihilation', all of which must therefore be vigorously affirmed. 'The tragic man', Nietzsche declares, 'affirms even the harshest suffering: he is sufficiently strong, rich, and capable of deifying to do so.'[10] Dionysus, god of tragedy, signifies pure *jouissance*, the unclean delights of the death drive, the bliss born of ecstatic, primordial pain. This exuberantly destructive power conjures up a galaxy of individual life forms only to bring them to ruin, thus demonstrating its own sublime imperishability. The tragic hero is a purely phenomenal creature, by whose death the unfathomable depths of the Dionysian remain serenely unruffled. He himself reaps a savage joy from his own destruction. To brood upon the price this ecstasy exacts in agony would be to capitulate to the degenerate consolations of compassion. A stiff dose of tragedy is the only hope for an ignoble Socratic age.

It is Christianity that this theory of tragedy has most clearly in its sights. For Nietzsche, it comes down to a question of Dionysus versus the Crucified. The 'god on the cross' revels in suffering for all the most morbid, ignoble of reasons. Christian morality, with its sickly rites of self-abnegation, represents a pure culture of the death drive, as self-torment is elevated to an ethics. 'The praise of the unselfish, self-sacrificing, virtuous person', he writes, '. . . has in any case not originated out of the spirit of unselfishness!'[11] In the *Twilight of the Idols*, Nietzsche speaks scathingly of Kant's moral philosophy as 'a sacrifice to the Moloch of abstraction'.[12] In a different sense, however, Nietzsche is not in the least averse to the idea of sacrifice. It is simply that for him it means not that one must be broken in order to be remade, but that others must be broken for one's own kind to flourish. Countless inferior types need to be oppressed, exploited and even exterminated for the Übermensch to thrive. One should harvest pleasure from the afflictions of others, rather than allow oneself to be infected by the loathsome virus of pity. Humanity as we have it is the product of a laborious process of sacrifice, of self-violation and self-crucifixion at its own craven, masochistic, guilt-ridden hands, but this living death will lay the groundwork for a sublime efflorescence of superior life in the future. Man as we know him, caught up in a vicious cycle of desire, trespass, guilt and self-loathing, shall be laid upon the altar so that a higher race may emerge. The most terrible sickness that has ever ravaged the human species – morality – will eventually be turned to life-enhancing ends. This whole horrific history, in which Man is disciplined, degutted and spiritually emasculated, reduced to a craven, docile, self-tormenting citizen, is in Nietzsche's view an essential condition for the advent of the Übermensch, he who will break free from the prison-house of ethics and legislate his own values in lordly disdain for the *canaille*. Sacrifice is to be justified by being historicised; but it also needs to be perpetuated in the present, as the sick, weak and degenerate are disposed of in the name of the progress of the species. If Christianity is to be reviled, Nietzsche argues in *The Will to Power*, it is among other things because of its sentimental demand that nobody should be offered up for the benefit of humanity as a whole. His own view is that genuine charity demands brutal suppression, against which the pseudo-humanitarianism of the Christian faith launches its pious protest. Indeed, progress can actually be measured by the degree of sacrifice it entails. If the French Revolution and its democratic-egalitarian aftermath are to be spurned, it is partly because there can be no possibility of sacrifice if all citizens are equal.

In contrast to this Social-Darwinist version of sacrifice, Nietzsche objects to what he sees as the cringing self-abasement of the Christian version, a grovelling which is in fact a cunningly masked *ressentiment*; but he is equally affronted by the claim that the Crucifixion has brought such sacrifice to a close. In his view, it represents the grotesque spectacle of God as creditor himself finally stepping in to relieve humanity of its debts.[13] If the cross renders sacrificial rites superfluous, it is because the Almighty engages in one of his most spectacularly omnipotent feats to date, bringing the whole grisly business of sin, guilt, punishment and obscene enjoyment to supreme consummation by taking over personal proprietorship of it. In homeopathic fashion, sacrifice is to be killed off by a lethal dose of its own medicine. It is abolished because God is powerful enough to pull off such a feat, not because his love and mercy render it redundant.

Nietzsche is mistaken to believe that Christianity finds value in suffering. On the contrary, Jesus never once counsels the diseased and disabled who flock around him to reconcile themselves to their misfortunes. Instead, in line with the mythology of his time, he seems to regard such afflictions as the work of Satan. In a fit of panic before his arrest, he himself prays to be released from his impending torture and death. If torment and death prove unavoidable, as in the case of the martyr, then it is a lesson of tragedy that to appropriate the inevitable, actively living one's self-dispossession to the end, can lay the groundwork for new life. To accept a self-divestment which is forced upon you is to seize the chance to convert it into the alternative self-abandonment of love. Jesus converts his destiny into his decision in just this sense, in the manner of the classical tragic protagonist. As Mary Douglas writes, 'When someone freely embraces the symbols of death, or death itself ... a great release of power for good should be expected to follow.'[14] It would be preferable, however, if one were not called upon to make any such grossly inconvenient display of moral courage in the first place. That it should prove necessary is itself a tragic affair, not a heaven-sent opportunity to flex one's moral muscles.

Jesus may be a tragic protagonist, but he is not portrayed as a heroic one. His desolate cry on the cross 'My God, my God, why hast thou forsaken me?' posits the existence of the Other only to call it mournfully or accusingly into question. It would appear that in his obdurate refusal to intervene, this frigidly remote Creator has confessed his true nullity, and in doing so has deprived Jesus's mission of a victorious outcome. Sacrifice, which traditionally pays homage to God's sovereignty, would seem in this instance to testify to either his impotence or his indifference. As Jürgen Moltmann argues, Jesus's lament (in fact, a quotation from a Psalm which like his own career ends on a rather more positive note) is among other things a plea that the Father should not bring discredit upon himself, testifying in his enigmatic silence to his own non-existence.[15] There would appear to be no support for Jesus's act in the Big Other, as the heavens remain ominously shut. His loving fidelity to his Father appears to meet with a chilling non-response. Like all authentic acts of faith, his self-surrender must thus be without an assured ground. Yet if it is groundless, it is also thus in the sense that the Father who sustains it is an unfathomable abyss of love rather than a copper-bottomed metaphysical guarantee. It is the Father himself who lies at the source of Jesus's faith, as the object-cause of his desire, and it is in this sense that he has not been forsaken. On the contrary, God is present on this scene as the power that enables Jesus to forsake himself.

The Father does indeed respond to his child – not as a voice from the heavens, but by raising him from the dead in contemptuous defiance of the powers of this world. As such, God is revealed in this murder mystery as the Other of the *nom du père* – as a form of transcendence in solidarity with failure and infirmity, and thus in revolt against the death-dealing Law that has brought his son to this pass. As G.K. Chesterton comments, 'That a good man may have his back to the wall is no more than we knew already, but that God could have His back to the wall is a boast for all insurgents for ever.'[16] Yahweh as sublime superego or custodian of the symbolic order is accordingly dethroned. The power that sustains Jesus's act of self-giving is the sworn adversary of the forces that do him to death, rather than their symbolic underwriting or Master Signifier. Yahweh's forgiveness, an act which falls entirely beyond the Law's comprehension, is in the words of C.F.D. Moule a 'radical, a drastic, a passionate and absolutely final acceptance of the terrible situation [of human criminality]'.[17] The oppressive patriarch in this scenario is not God but the imperial Roman state and its satraps. What Jesus calls his Father may be impenetrable in its purpose (why is it allowing this terrible thing to happen?), but it is also the desire at the centre of his own being, which is part of what is meant by calling Jesus the Son of God; and to yield to the desire which constitutes one's being is to be free. The Father is not subject to a title or image. He is to be known only through the gift of faith. The only palpable icon of this deity is the ignominious collapse of Calvary, rather as the only true image of the future is the failure of the present. Jesus's loyalty to the scum of the earth, along with his reduction to so much dead meat on the cross, deflates the transferential illusions of those who would see in the Father a *sujet supposé à savoir*. Perhaps a touch incongruously, God's silence on Calvary may be compared to the silence of the psychoanalyst who refuses the role of Big Other or transcendental guarantor. It is this refusal of the consoling word – of any rhetoric of restitution or specious promise of paradise – that punctures all fantasies of plenitude and throws Jesus back purely upon his faith. In accepting the non-existence of the Big Other, making the death of this satanic image of God its own, the subject assumes its own vacuity, accepting the fact that his identity is grounded in nothing more than his loving loyalty. It is this vacuity that is 'literalised' in its death. As Eric Santner writes, 'We should say, then, that that socialised human animal is susceptible to the force of truth only because his or her animality or creatureliness has been heightened by the impact of an anxiety-filled encounter with a void.'[18]

Slavoj Žižek follows Jacques Lacan in viewing sacrifice as an attempt to fill in the alarming incompleteness of the Other, disavowing its lack in order to sustain a fantasy of it as omnipotent and self-consistent.[19] It is this fetishism, or fantasy of repletion, which underlies the practice of idolatry. That God should be lacking or symbolically castrated is not to be tolerated. Nor can one easily embrace a deity who presents himself as suffering flesh and blood, and whose familiarity is thus likely to breed contempt. For instance, an embarrassment about God's pathetic vulnerability is a staple motif of Graham Greene's fiction. If one is to have a deity at all, one should surely opt for the kind who will make one feel agreeably chastised. There is no point in settling for a spineless, hopelessly open-minded, perpetually vacillating God. The intolerable weakness of Yahweh, his unfathomable love and mercy, must accordingly be masked by a paranoid image of him as patriarch and sovereign power. He can then loom up as adversary and accuser (the meaning of the Hebrew word 'Satan'), relieving us of our guilt by punishing our transgressions, and affording us the obscene pleasures of self-mortification in the process. To refuse such idolatry is to claim along with Lacan that the Big Other is a fraud. Atheists and believers can at least agree on this. God is not a formidably powerful creature, which is why he cannot be sweet-talked or soft-soaped, and why sacrifice is accordingly superfluous. Because Yahweh is revealed on the cross as friend, lover and fellow victim, the image of him as hungry for appeasement is overturned, and with it the necessity for ritual oblation. There is no need to slaughter animals in the name of some higher spiritual power, since this God is an animal himself. If idolatry is proscribed by the Hebrew Scriptures, it is because the only image of Yahweh is human flesh and blood. It is his carnal compassion for those of his own kind that shatters the image of him as an imperious overlord to be placated. Once one recognises in the coming of the Son the coming of the Father, the Law yields ground to forgiveness and sacrifice is rendered superfluous. It is in the abyssal depths of the human subject, a nothingness which rebuffs all representation, that the negativity of the godhead is to be glimpsed.

Žižek writes of the passage from tragedy to comedy as one from a situation in which one's identity is guaranteed by a Master Signifier – a form of sovereignty that lends meaning and consistency to one's life, but to which one tragically fails to be equal – to a condition in which any such support is lacking. Instead, in its transition from the sublime to the ridiculous, the comic subject is sustained by its identification with the *objet petit a* – with some surplus fragment, traumatic kernel or trifling piece of the Real that subverts all symbolic identifications.[20] Jesus himself is the bit of trash or excremental remainder that the symbolic order proves unable to accommodate and thus expels as so much garbage, but which in its very abjection exposes that order's lacunae and limitations. In doing so, it also discloses the possibility of a new dispensation, as the revolutionary Passover from the old to the new transforms the coordinates of the existing symbolic order. One might say of the crucified Jesus that in 'tragic' mode he lives up to the demand of the Father or Master Signifier precisely in his 'comic' failure, since it is this, rather than tragic heroism, that is demanded of him. It is in falling short of tragic nobility that he is equal to the Father's desire. Instead, he becomes nothing, a condition in which the highest and the lowest coincide. What escapes the symbolic order is what is too trivial to be represented there, but also too sublime. Only by being reduced to negativity can Jesus become an authentic sign of the godhead. Only by being flayed and mutilated can he fully assume the role of Son of God. 'You want to be like a god? You mean you really want to be crucified?' is the sick joke of the Christian Gospel.

Like all agents of a revolutionary act, Jesus must undergo a radical self-divestiture as a subject. The subjects of baptism undergo a similar self-destitution in symbolic form, exposed to the trauma of the death drive through ritual drowning and as such able to convert this radical negativity into a new creation. Jesus speaks of his death as his baptism. Only through this encounter with *thanatos*, at the utmost limit of human experience, can a truth event be opened up, one which involves a momentous emptying and renaming of the subject of this perilous act of passage. It can now be seen in retrospect that Jesus, a man notably wary of all titles and designations, an empty signifier rebuffing all incriminating or well-meaning attempts to pin a label on him, is to be identified as the Christ. For his disciples, everyday ranks, distinctions and identities are thus dissolved. To heed the summons of the cross is to refuse one's allotted place in the symbolic order in response to a Real that shears through it like a sword.[21] Jesus has come to tear one family member from the other in the name of his mission. The distinction that matters now is one between those who are faithful to his word, and who are therefore at risk of being butchered by the state, and those who remain in thrall to the powers of darkness: exploiters, militarists, media barons, money-grubbers, power-mongers, smooth-talking ideologues and the like. The transformative action of the Real springs from the lacks and fissures of the symbolic order, signified above all by the *anawim* or dispossessed with whom Jesus throws in his lot. When Paul speaks of Christ's followers as the scourings and leftovers of the earth, it is this he has in mind. As a type of the *anawim* himself, homeless, vagrant, without property, partner or profession, Jesus incarnates in his lifestyle the vacuity of the Real at the core of the symbolic.

44

One might say of Jesus, as Jacques Derrida says of Abraham, that 'having renounced winning, expecting neither response nor recompense, expecting nothing that can be *given back* to him . . . [he] sees that God gives back to him, in the instant of absolute renunciation, the very thing that he had already, in the same instant, decided to sacrifice.'[22] 'Jesus, for the sake of his fellow men and women', writes Herbert McCabe, 'accepted total failure, death and crucifixion and left it all to the will of the Father.'[23] As Jean-Luc Marion comments of the artist, 'he first gives himself, without ever knowing in advance if he will lose himself or be saved.'[24] 'The contradiction here', remarks Søren Kierkegaard in *The Sickness Unto Death*, 'is that in human terms the undoing is certain and yet there is still possibility.' 'The tragic hero', he writes in *Fear and Trembling*, 'gives up the certain for the even more certain';[25] what he calls the knight of faith, by contrast, feels no such solid foundations beneath his feet. Like Abraham commanded to slay his son, he stands solitary and bereft, burdened with a faith which in rational terms is bound to appear offensive and absurd. Only if the cross is lived in tragic resignation as final and absolute might it cease to be either. Only by living one's death to the full, rather than treating it as a springboard to eternity, might it prove possible to transcend it. It is thus unwise to speak of sacrifice as refusing the reality of death.[26] Ernst Bloch writes of the communist martyr that his 'Good Friday is not mitigated or even cancelled out by an Easter Sunday on which he personally will be re-awakened to life.'[27] But neither is this true of Jesus, whose risen body continues to manifest the marks of his torture and death.

This is not the viewpoint of a Schlegel or a Nietzsche. Tragedy for them moves in a realm remote from the rape of a child or the collapse of a coal mine. On the contrary, it represents a kind of secular theodicy. If one bows submissively to one's suffering, it is only in the same instant to be raised up in glory. Destruction is more blissful than calamitous. There can be no genuine loss in this excessively replete vision. Dionysus versus the Crucified represents a conflict between two different versions of tragedy, in which what is ultimately at stake is the reality of human affliction. Those who are crucified are likely to take suffering rather more seriously than gods for whom being torn limb from limb is a matter of exuberant self-affirmation. The legend of Christ's descent into hell after his crucifixion is designed to put paid to such callow triumphalism. It is an abandonment to the terror and non-sense of the death drive. Here, hell signifies the dissolution of meaning and value into cackles of nihilistic laughter, along with a vision of humanity as so much shit. Unless Jesus's redemptive action can encompass these obscene sniggers, buffoonish yelps and demonic howls of mockery, it is worthless. What can be heard in these guffaws is what Jacques Lacan calls *les non-dupes*, those whose illusion is to believe that they have seen through all meaning as an illusion. Jesus, to adopt a phrase from Slavoj Žižek, must accept the Real in all its brute meaninglessness – an idiocy that springs from the impasse and implosion of the symbolic order which his death signifies.

* * *

There must, to be sure, be law; but as long as this is a necessity, there is always the possibility of making a fetish or idol out of it, as those under its sway come to desire the Law itself, falling morbidly in love with its seductive sadism and obeying it purely on account of its formal authority rather than craving the justice it demands. It is the difference between *agape* and *eros* – between those who practise the charity commanded by the Mosaic Law and those who become erotically entangled in its death-dealing toils, knowing nothing of it but its cruel, superegoic underside. To be enslaved by the Law is to revel in the self-lacerating delight it forces us to reap from our submission to its power. The obscene supplement or excess of the Law can be seen in the way it solicits its own transgression, but it is also to be found in its alluring invitation to love it for its own sake (for the Law, after all, is the Law) in the very act of issuing its peremptory commands.

Rather as the Law is awash with desire in its vindictive campaign to bring us to nothing, so, conversely, desire itself can become ritualised and automated, assuming all the coercive, anonymous force of a law. If Freud names this condition neurosis, Paul gives it the title of sin, which he regards as a matter of the unconscious. When I sin, he writes in Romans, 'I do not understand my own actions'. The sinful subject is a split subject. To sin is to be decentred or self-divided, an enigma to oneself, as one's most reputable intentions are derailed by forces that cannot be controlled and of which one is a mere helpless function. Because sin is in this sense impersonal, it can be countered only by a power (grace) which also springs from beyond the subject, rather as neurotic behaviour can be altered not by an act of will but by changes that reach deep into the unconscious. 'Flesh' (*sarx*) is the name Paul gives to the monstrously impersonal drives he calls sin, as opposed to the body (*soma*), which in his view is holy. Sin is perhaps best seen as a form of addiction. It signifies the body out of control, self-divided, a prey to its own neurotic compulsions and repetitions, to desires that have grown mechanical, obtuse and despotic. Sin is a form of false consciousness that prevents us from being aware of our true desire, which for both Thomas Aquinas (who sees it as a desire for God) and Jacques Lacan (for whom it is a desire of and for the Real) represents the fundamental law of one's being.

Paul connects sin with death, though one might speak more appropriately in this context of the death drive. In Lacan's view, what prevents us from accepting death is less our attachment to life than a kind of blind, indestructible urge to persist in our existence, which can be called either libido or the death drive, and of which Arthur Schopenhauer's horrifying Will is the supreme image. It is this grisly parody of immortality that deprives us of the capacity to die, and the sinful are those who inhabit this liminal, zombie-like zone between life and death, incapable of embracing their mortality (which for Christian faith would be the condition of eternal life) and thus condemned to a living death that knows no end. Because it represents a form of ersatz immortality, the death drive is hostile to the body – to the local, sensuous and particularised, to the organic and reproductive, to love and sexuality – which it can see only as so many fleshly obstacles to its own futile, compulsive, virulently abstract persistence. When this hostility takes the form of wishing to annihilate the sensuous, organic and affective as scandals and offences in their own right, we can justly begin to speak of evil.[28]

This is not a condition from which the Law can redeem us. On the contrary, it seals our self-division by stoking our self-loathing. Indeed, it is the Law which in singling out certain actions by its prohibitions allows our desire to become perversely fixated upon them. It is thus caught in a performative contradiction. Like the superego, source of moral conscience, the Law has its invaluable aspects, not least since what it teaches is unequivocally good. We are not to murder, kidnap (the probable source of the prohibition against stealing), hijack the sexual partners of others and so on. Yet the Law cannot proscribe these practices without advertising their perpetual possibility, thus inciting the very offences it condemns. In this sense, it is perverse to the core. Like psychoanalysis in the view of the satirist Karl Kraus, it is part of the problem to which it proffers a solution. Though it is blameless in itself, it resembles the kind of grossly inadequate parent who can do no more than rub our noses in where we go wrong. If it can castigate vice, it cannot persuade us to virtue.

This is not to deny that it is a useful device for the moral tenderfoot, even if it proves superfluous for those who have spiritually come of age. The Law is a ladder to be kicked away once we have mounted it. In Paul's view, those who receive the Spirit through faith have no need of a moral textbook, since they perform through love what those enslaved by the Law undertake out of obligation. They are thus absolved from the guilt, self-hatred and masochistic pleasure which spring from falling short of the Law's imperious demands, and to this extent are less in thrall to *thanatos*. Offering oneself up to the Law in the guise of a burnt offering always involves the secret joy of a vicarious self-dismembering. 'We violate no body so much as our own', comments V.S. Naipaul in *The Mimic Men*, 'towards it we display the perversity of the cat that constantly rips its wounds open'. Rather than annulling the Law, the Spirit transforms its dead letter into an active way of life. What is overthrown by this dispensation of grace is not the content of Law, which is to be commended, but its form – which is to say, the Law as the demonic repetition of the death drive. The fact that it cannot work without forcing men and women to wield the knife against themselves is where the Law is most plainly cursed, to use Paul's own description of it. This is why, once the Law yields to the Spirit, the whole apparatus of ritual sacrifice can be set aside.

The command to love is as ruthlessly anonymous and impersonal as any law. It is not at the mercy of specific persons, cultures, sentiments or occasions. Whatever Hegel may have considered, we are not speaking of replacing the Judaic Law with a subjective purity of heart.[29] Only a desire that has passed through the anonymity of death can figure as that alternative form of anonymity which is the love of strangers. Only thus might it prove a match for the equally anonymous forces of injustice, whose sources are for the most part institutional rather than individual. The violence of Calvary is a case in point. Nobody in this blood-soaked scenario can really be said to be responsible for it. Jesus himself did not seek his death, though he did not resist it either. The Jewish ruling class were no doubt understandably fearful that this alarmingly popular preacher might trigger an insurrection, which would bring the full ferocity of Roman power down on the heads of their people. The Roman governor, Pontius Pilate, whitewashed by the Gospel writers for their own political ends, had a history of corruption and brutality for which he was finally dismissed from the Roman service, but he would doubtless have regarded it as his duty to quell dissent.

* * *

A key moment in the evolution of sacrifice arrives when the victim themselves becomes conscious of their condition, and in doing so assumes agency of the event. We are now en route from goats and sheaves of grain to the consciousness of the tragic hero. What was a process to be endured becomes a project to be executed. Those who are cast out can now be signs of the criminal nature of the status quo, and by making this destiny their own can become the cornerstone of a new dispensation. We begin, then, with a vulnerable victim, who in a further phase of development rises to a sense of their own infirmity; next, they appropriate this infirmity as the truth of their condition, and in the act of so doing can embark on a transition to power. When it becomes a matter of voluntary self-giving, the institution of sacrifice crosses over from Nature to culture, myth to tragedy, cult and ritual to ethics and politics. One might even claim that it foreshadows its own future in this respect. Robin Lane Fox reports that the ancient Greeks would sprinkle the sacrificial beast with water to cause it to shiver, a motion that was taken as a gesture of assent to its own slaughter.[30] For the ancient Romans, writes Carlin Barton, 'the more actively voluntary, the more effective the sacrifice'.[31] The soldier or gladiator who swears an oath to be slain exalts himself in that act, establishing 'the debased and humiliated as highly charged, as dangerous'.[32] Those who live at the point of death are to be approached warily, in fear and trembling.

So much may be acceptable to the theologians, but it is scarcely commonplace among secular theorists of sacrifice. On the contrary, there is a consensus among them that the custom is primarily a conservative one. There are, to be sure, exceptions. One of the strikingly few theorists of sacrifice to grasp it in subversive terms is Georges Bataille, who treats it as a form of de-reification, liberating objects from their customary social uses in the manner of the avant-garde artist for a revolutionary new order of meaning. Divested of their mundane functions, these things become forms of useless, unreserved, unconditional expenditure, and as such constitute an affront to bourgeois utility. The sacred represents a critique of instrumental rationality. Objects are transferred from the sphere of labour and exchange value to the domain of the intimate, subjective, erotic, luxurious and gratuitous, so that the sacrificial rite re-enacts the political passage from the kingdom of necessity to the realm of freedom. Sacrifice belongs to a 'world of uncalculated and violent generosity',[33] and Bataille sees its cult of total, instant consumption as a rebuff to the deferred gratifications of capitalist productivity. Death destroys the false, commodified identity of things, and in an ecstatic strike against time lays bare the essence of eternity at their heart. Since authentic human existence is eternal, death is its most appropriate image. As Bataille comments, 'death reveals life in its plenitude and dissolves the real order'.[34] As in tragic art, the annihilation of the finite reveals by contrast the brooding presence of boundlessness.[35]

For most authors, though, the purpose of the rite is far from subversive. Instead, it aims to placate a range of potentially destructive powers; buttress and integrate the social order (not least in the face of some disruption or turbulent transition); maintain some precious continuity with the origins of the tribe; renew the sources of divine energy which sustain human existence; and redress the delicate equilibrium between humanity and the cosmos. Piously performed, sacrifice can fend off catastrophe and even prevent the universe from collapsing. As such, in the words of one scholar, it is 'the supreme gesture without which humanity would perish'.[36] The refusal of the early Christians to make sacrifice to pagan gods was thought to imperil the state. Indeed, it was the primary reason for their persecution.[37] It was in order to defend them from the charge that their recusancy was responsible for the fall of Rome that Augustine wrote *The City of God*. Christians were martyred for refusing to bow the knee to the superstitions of the secular authorities, which is to say for elevating the things that are God's – justice, mercy, caring for the poor and the like – over the things that are Caesar's. The early Christians refused to acknowledge the sovereignty of the Roman Empire by offering pagan sacrifice, and thus occasionally became sacrificial offerings (or martyrs) themselves.

Theorists are not mistaken in seeing many of the functions of sacrifice as preservative of the established order. 'Political power cannot be exercised without sacrificial practice', writes Marcel Detienne.

> To found a colony it is sufficient to bring a spit from the home country and a pot with fire in it. The sacrifice thus made possible is not only the act of founding a new political community born of the first. It will become the basis for the filial relations maintained by a colony with its mother city.[38]

By ritually incorporating the icons of death, the tribe achieves a symbolic victory over this calamity and secures a kind of immortality for its social order. Death, observes J.H.M. Beattie, 'is in some sense an anomaly, a disruption, a breach of social order',[39] and sacrifice may be a way to restore the stability it undermines. Yet we have also seen how such breaches and disruptions can release profoundly transformative powers. There is a case for claiming that Christianity is the point at which sacrifice becomes subversive in just this sense. Every political regime stands under the judgement of the cross.

Like a host of other commentaries, Malcolm Bull's *Seeing Things Hidden* regards sacrifice as necessarily supportive of the status quo. So does René Girard's *Violence and the Sacred*, for which the mimetic nature of human desire results in a murderous rivalry which only the victimising of the scapegoat can resolve.[40] The violence that human beings unleash on each other's heads can thus be displaced onto the blameless body of the scapegoat, whose death or expulsion then purges this chronic aggression. Since the *pharmakos* is a mongrel-ised, undifferentiated animal, the primary signifier of moral and social disorder, the act of putting it to death re-establishes hierarchy and stability. It is in this sense that social cohesion is founded on an act of destruction. In Girard's view, it is this ritual mechanism that the New Testament will finally demystify and denounce, as the execution of the innocent Jesus, the latest of the sacrificial victims, lays bare its barbarism and brutal injustice. The only cure for violence is Christianity. With the Crucifixion, the perspective shifts from an ideology that holds that sacrifice or scapegoating is essential to the maintenance of social order, to a solidarity with those victimised by it. Unmasked for the abomination it is, the savage pre-history of sacrifice gives way to the story of modern civilisation. Love, at least in principle, replaces mutual hostility.

The problems with this formidably influential case are too many to examine fully. Yet a few critical comments are in order. It is hard for this account to make sense of the clear endorsement of sacrifice to be found in Hebrews; but Girard, who apparently regards himself as a finer theologian than the author of that epistle, issues a stern rebuke to it in his *Things Hidden since the Foundation of the World*. In some of his earlier writings, he sees the sacrificial view of Calvary only as involving the unleashing of a capricious violence on the part of a jealous God. He thus fails to recognise that the God of Calvary is himself a violent transgressor who brings to grief the powers of this world by substituting flesh and blood for their sterile sway. It is divine law that is politically disruptive, and human edicts which are death-dealing. Besides, if the Gospel does not simply disown sacrifice in an access of liberal enlightenment, it is because in a world that finds justice both offensive and inconvenient, events of this kind are likely to prove tragically unavoidable. Girard, who fully acknowledges the Christian commitment to the poor, sees in his own way that faith involves a disruptive bringing to bear of the Crucifixion on the spurious stability of civilisation. It is just that he does not draw any clear political and historical conclusions from this insight. For a thinker hailed as the most eminent theorist of sacrifice of our time, this would seem rather a sizeable blind spot, though one would scarcely gather so from the hagiographic accounts of his acolytes.[41]

Girard's view of violence as invariably mimetic, a matter of desiring the desire of the other, is drastically reductive. Nor is mimetic desire always as destructive as he imagines. In this bleakly Hobbesian vision, human aggression is assigned a single archaic cause, with scant attention to the role of material interests, political conflicts or social contradictions. The First World War, for example, is on this account not primarily a clash of competing national capitals but yet another effect of scapegoating, to be treated in much the same terms as the ritual cannibalism of the Tupinambá tribe of Brazil. As in most mythological schemas, history is violently elided. It is worth noting that this conservative viewpoint, for which material history simply rings the changes on certain abiding principles, should be coupled in Girard's work with a patrician disdain for the 'mob'.[42] There is little sense of violence as structural and systemic – as 'rational', in a somewhat anaemic sense of the term – rather than as some primordial force injuriously at work beneath the paucity of reason. The vital relation between violence and material scarcity goes largely unexamined. Tragedy, scapegoating and sacrifice are too hastily conflated.

The Girardian claim that the scapegoat mechanism is the generative principle of all culture is absurdly hyperbolic. Can every social institution really be explained in terms of the lynch mob swooping upon its hapless victim? Scapegoating becomes a portentous 'theory of everything', a King Charles's head or Casaubon-like key to all mythologies. Girard is right to claim that crime and bloodshed lie at the origin of civilisation, but not all of these atrocities involve scapegoating, or can be resolved in that ritual fashion. Nor are peace and unity always the undoubted benefits he seems to assume. Appeals for unity are issued often enough by those whose selfish interests it may serve. Some contradictions are indispensable, just as some conflicts may be life-yielding.[43] They are not to be treated in naively progressivist style simply as noxious and negative. Girard's condemnation of violence is lacking in nuance – a grand moral gesture bought at the cost of historical specificity. Love, he claims, is a 'form of transcendence that never acts by means of violence, is never responsible for any violence and remains radically opposed to violence'.[44] The statement invites too easy an assent. It is not only that violence may need to be deployed in defence of the innocent; it is also that in conditions of injustice, love and violence are likely to prove indissociable, as the practice of martyrdom testifies. Nor can acts of love always control their potentially destructive consequences.

Sacrifice, then, has by no means been superannuated, even if the ritual version of the practice has indeed been largely routed. To imagine so is to overlook the history of modern martyrdom. To see the custom in orthodox Enlightenment fashion purely as a species of savagery – one now thankfully consigned by liberal modernity to the ashcan of history – is not only complacent. It is also to grasp sacrifice for the most part in the specialised sense of scapegoating, rather than in some more positive or political light. In Girard's view, the Crucifixion reinterprets sacrifice as moral obscenity, and by exposing it as such brings it to a close. Sacrifice must now be judged as nothing but moral atrocity. The more radical point, however, is that Jesus's death reinterprets an atrocious political murder precisely *as sacrifice* – as a disruptive transitus from death to life, and thus as a sign, promise and agent of human emancipation. Girard shows a proper compassion for the sacrificial victim; but he is less vigilant to the way in which that victim, by incarnating the violence of the social order, can appropriate and transform it.

In a bracing critique of Girard's thought, John Milbank questions his essentialising of sacrifice, pointing out that not all such practices are regarded as dangerous or ambiguous; that they are not always associated à la Girard with scapegoating or the suppression of social conflict; that they do not invariably involve self-abandonment, the expulsion of some alien element or the payment of a debt, and so on.[45] One might add to the charge sheet Girard's habit of raiding literary works for their conceptual content with scant regard for their formal properties. One might note, too, that his account is remarkably innocent of the concept of social class, as bankers and garbage collectors engage as equal players in a game governed by an abstract universal logic of rivalry, scapegoating and mimesis. There are other forms of social division of which he is equally heedless. Girard, a thinker of remarkable ambition and originality, is without doubt the most eminent theorist of sacrifice of modern times, but his vision of the institution is in the end too monocular to allow for its prodigal variety. The signal virtue of his work is that it succeeds in placing this unpopular practice squarely back on the intellectual agenda, thus challenging an entrenched modern orthodoxy; its notable flaw is that it serves to confirm those orthodox perceptions of the custom as merely barbaric. To counter this viewpoint, we must go on to look more closely at the institution of martyrdom.

Chapter 3

MARTYRDOM AND MORTALITY

AMONG THE MANY duties included under the heading of knowing how to live, writes Michel de Montaigne, is the business of knowing how to die.[1] It belongs to that knowledge to recognise that death is not to be feared in the way that one might fear injury or bankruptcy. These are experiences we have to live with; but though we also have to live with the fact of our mortality, we do not by definition live with death itself. What we fear is not so much being dead, which as Lucretius argues in *De Rerum Natura* is nothing in itself and so nothing to be afraid of, as the absolute loss of experience it entails. It is not death that is alarming, in short, but the prospect of no longer being alive. This is not, to be sure, the only aspect of mortality we find unsettling. As Samuel Scheffler points out, the thought that one will at some point simply lapse from existence is strange enough to induce a kind of panic or vertigo.[2] One of the signal advantages of being dead, however, is that it puts paid to this vertigo altogether. Death is the one problem that we can be certain will be resolved, being in homeopathic manner the infallible cure for the anxieties it engenders. It will simply be wiped from our minds as our minds are wiped away.

Death is sometimes presented as a journey or voyage into the unknown, yet this is ironic, since (if one sets aside suicide or martyrdom) it involves doing nothing at all. It requires no technical skill, intensive rehearsal or specialised knowledge, strangely for such an intensely dramatic occasion. If it is indeed a journey, one is in the position of a passenger lounging below deck, not the captain on the bridge. At what is perhaps the most momentous point in our lives, we are entirely passive. This is one reason why death may pose more of a scandal to modern social orders than to pre-modern ones, since they are more accustomed to being masters of their own destinies. There are other societies for which death consummates a powerlessness manifest in everyday life, and in this sense can be said to signify something of the truth of everyday existence. Generally speaking, there is more continuity between life and death for the poor than for the prosperous.

Dying is the process by which nothingness as *néant* – as some fearful enigma or obscurely apprehended horror – turns into nothingness as simple *rien*. We are converted from subjects to objects in the twinkling of an eye. It is the consequences of this that are so disquieting. No longer to be alive is objectionable in much the same way that one might feel uneasy about being anaesthetised – not because it is unpleasant in itself, but because it involves missing out on experiences that are pleasant in themselves, and for rather longer than the duration of a surgical operation.[3] The fact that one may live on in public memory, or through one's progeny or accomplishments, is meagre compensation for this loss. As Woody Allen remarked, 'I don't want to live on in the hearts of my countrymen. I want to live on in my apartment.'

It is not because life is supremely valuable that death is a problem. A martyr does not regard her existence as more precious than whatever she yields it up for. People who live in atrocious pain may well feel that dying would be preferable to existing. The philosopher Thomas Nagel disputes this view, considering as he does that 'life is worth living even when the bad elements of experience are plentiful, and the good ones too meagre to outweigh the bad ones on their own.'[4] What tips the balance, he believes, is our sheer capacity for experience, rather than any of its particular contents. But it is surely doubtful whether being capable of enduring agony for years on end outweighs the negativity of the pain itself. It is no more true that the capacity to experience is a value in itself than that, as the fraudulent old cliché has it, all experience is valuable. Being burnt alive is not generally regarded as worth experiencing, rather as simply to be alive is not always adequate recompense for a wretched existence. There are those who insist on the preciousness of the fact that I am irreplaceably myself, whatever afflictions this may involve. I may make a mess of my life, but at least it is uniquely mine. But many people would probably have been better off being someone else. Hermann Göring, for example.

There are a good many human lives that, though free of chronic physical suffering, have little to recommend them. There are plenty of people who would probably have been better off never being born, as Schopenhauer is audacious enough to acknowledge. No doubt there are those among the countless millions of men and women who have spent lives of semi-destitution and backbreaking toil who may have felt that their existence had its redeeming features, but probably only just. Perhaps one of the few advantages of such a life is to make the business of dying rather less formidable, just as it is easier to abandon the world if one imagines a future in which men and women will have advertisements regularly flashed on their brains. A less dismal way to ease one's dying, one recommended by the Christian Gospel, is to live selflessly. It is those who cling to their identities like a drowning man to a piece of driftwood who find it difficult or impossible to die, as William Golding's Pincher Martin discovers to his cost. The Christian doctrines of purgatory and hell concern just this. Even then, however, one cannot avoid the thought of the distress one's death will bring to others, a grief to which the selfless are peculiarly sensitive. The most effective way to die would thus be to combine a lifetime of service to others with a steadfast avoidance of intimate relationships, a condition known as, among other things, the monastic life.

What death cuts short is not an inherent value (life), but the possibility of such value. Being alive is a necessary but not sufficient condition of enjoying a worthwhile existence. It is an indispensable precondition for reading Proust or drinking malt whisky. Because these are agreeable ways of passing the time, there is no reason why one should not wish to pursue them indefinitely. There seems no pressing reason why they should come to an end, any more than there is any compelling reason for taking them up in the first place. The gratuitous doesn't need to exist, but nor does it need not to. There is no natural closure to activities of this kind, no logical term to them, which is what makes their being cut off seem so unreasonable. There is nothing about them that suggests they need to end. It is not as though they are organic processes which emerge, rise to some fruitful consummation, degenerate, grow obsolescent and wither away. They are not the kind of things that can be used up, run out of steam, wither on the branch or find themselves on their last legs. As Nagel comments, the eventual disappearance of our inner world is 'not the realisation of a possibility already contained in the conception of it', as is the case with our bodies.[5] Because pursuits like friendship and breeding hamsters are gratuitous, they seem in principle capable of going on for ever. The fact that one cannot engage in such activities in perpetuity is thus something of an outrage. Yet if the gratuitousness of these things means not seeing why they should come to a conclusion, it also means that there is no cast-iron way of justifying them, and thus of launching a cogent case for them to continue. One might imagine being spared in order to save a child from drowning, but not in order to reread Hölderlin or polish off the remnants of the Merlot.

All the same, the issue continues to rankle. If one can spend fifty years delighting in Verdi or witty banter, why not five million? One reason why not, advanced by the philosopher Bernard Williams, involves what one might call the argument from utter tedium. Wouldn't even the most dedicated narcissist baulk at the prospect of being stuck with himself with no end in sight, a condition traditionally associated with hell?[6] There are also those for whom the idea of immortality after death is equally dreadful. For the Kierkegaard of *The Sickness Unto Death*, it is possible to believe that there is such a life yet devoutly wish there were not, daunted by the prospect of having to labour tirelessly in this world for one's salvation in the next. A limitless life in this world, Williams claims, would also be a meaningless one. In his essay 'Science as Vocation', Max Weber sees the keynote of Leo Tolstoy's thought as the claim that the notion of infinite progress has robbed death of its meaning, since we can now never die fulfilled. There is always more futurity to be launched upon. All the same, it might be possible to settle for half and request, say, a modest millennium rather than an exorbitant infinity, perhaps punctuated by spells of drug-induced oblivion when time begins to weigh heavily on one's hands. Nagel points out that though we speak of Keats's death at the age of twenty-five as tragic, but not the death of Tolstoy at the age of eighty-two, the latter would seem almost equally lamentable if the average human life-span were a thousand years. It is worth noting that Williams, who mistakenly tends to use the terms 'eternal' and 'immortal' interchangeably, speaks at one point of *eternal* life as boring, which surely cannot be so.[7] There is no time to be bored in eternity because there is no time. The Christian idea of heaven involves not immortality in the sense of life without end, but the transcendence of time itself. This is why it is not a question of an 'afterlife', in the sense of an infinite stretch of time in the wake of one's death. Besides, 'afterlife' or 'survival' also suggests a placid continuity with the present, which for Christianity is not the best way of trying to grasp the cataclysmic event of the transformation of the flesh.

The theologian John Macquarrie compares human life to a piece of music. 'If that piece of music just went on and on indefinitely', he comments, 'it would have no form or meaning or beauty.'[8] No doubt there are those who would prefer to be formless, meaningless, ugly and alive. Besides, that something has an end does not necessarily endow it with a form. The alphabet has an end, but no discernible shape. Samuel Scheffler is another who believes that death lends our lives much of their form and meaning, and that the desire for immortality is consequently misplaced. 'Our ability to lead value-laden lives', he writes, 'is not only compatible with the fact that we will die but actually depends on it . . . My own death bends my life into a significant arc.'[9] That human lives should be bounded, as well as that they should proceed in certain definitive stages, is in Scheffler's view essential to them. Besides, he argues, many of our values depend on protection from disease, harm and danger, which themselves depend in turn on the prospect of death; and it is our awareness that time is scarce which impels us to evaluate in the first place, elevating certain goods over others. It is not clear, however, that value depends as weightily as Scheffler considers either on the threat of its negation or on the constraints of temporality. He is right, as we shall see, to claim that 'we need to die in order to live',[10] but not in the sense he has in mind.

Wanting to live for ever is not necessarily a question of greed. To be greedy is to want more than your fair share, but there is no having one's fair share of lying by the ocean or playing the clarinet. It may be, as the Epicureans teach, that one should savour such pleasures in moderation, but there seems no reason why one should not practise moderation for all eternity – it could even be a way of getting rather good at it. It may help to assuage our dismay at the impossibility of such eternal delights, however, that even the more functional, apparently essential features of our life have just as little foundation as the more obviously decorative aspects. In fact, there is no necessity to our existence as a whole, a fact that when applied to the cosmos at large is known as the doctrine of Creation. The doctrine concerns not the fact that the world came into existence, but that it did not need to. There are, to be sure, certain necessary features of it – physical laws, for example – but they might always have been different, or not have existed at all. For the idea of Creation, a certain contingency or gratuitousness lies at the heart even of necessity. We should be grateful even for a single moment of existence, then, since there might just as easily have been nothing. Death is the final, humiliating confirmation that the universe, far from owing us a living, has no regard for us whatsoever. Stephen Mulhall has written of seeing each thing in the world as if the world as a whole were their backdrop, but this is not to see them as grounded in some cosmic necessity.[11] On the contrary, he means seeing them as sharing in the radical contingency of Creation itself. Only by thus acknowledging their perishability can we truly savour their value, like the mournfully, orgasmically burst grape of Keats's 'Ode to Melancholy'.

All the same, it is not entirely unreasonable to believe that one might live for ever. If human existence were a field with visible frontiers or precipitous edges, the idea that one might simply keep ploughing ahead, with no grand finale in sight, would seem mere wishful thinking. Yet since there are no such boundaries to one's existence as grasped from the inside, it seems capable of stretching endlessly away on all sides. Even the most shapely of biographies or doggedly purposeful of careers remains blurred at the edges and mired in contingency. It is an open text rather than an achieved artefact. 'Our life', writes Ludwig Wittgenstein, 'has no end in just the way our visual field has no limits', and the moment of the end of life is not for Wittgenstein something we can experience.[12] It is true that these limits may begin to make themselves felt in old age, as one's strength starts to fail and mortality makes its presence felt as an internal frontier. For the body to be mortal means for it to bear its ultimate undoing within itself. Giuseppe Tomasi di Lampedusa writes in his novel *The Leopard* of a young couple for whom death is 'not an experience which pierced the marrow of their bones', simply an event that happened to others. For the young, death is more like a rumour of insurrection in a foreign land than a disease brewing in the blood. They do not see the self-loss it entails as prefigured here and now in the lack that is desire, or in the ceaseless act of negation by which the human subject projects itself into a future. They are not especially conscious that 'we carr[y] our death within us as a fruit bears its kernel', as Rainer Maria Rilke writes in *The Notebooks of Malte Laurids Brigge*.

Yet even this literal internalising of one's mortality is not enough to throw one's existence as a whole into relief. It is the fact that life cannot be totalised that makes death seem so unreal, since there is no perceptible frontier beyond which it might be lurking. Gianni Vattimo remarks in *The End of Modernity* that the human subject can grasp itself as a whole only in relation to the event of its ceasing to be, which is to say that it can found itself only upon its groundlessness, but it is surely doubtful that the thought of death lends coherence to one's life in this sense.[13] Besides, our identities are too much in the keeping of the Other for them to figure as integral for ourselves, and thus for us to have any very clear sense of their finitude. At the same time, the lack of self-possession that results from being in the custodianship of the Other is a foretaste of death itself. Celebrity, which can bring with it the sense of an outside to oneself that eludes one's grasp, intensifies this sense of non-self-identity and as such allows one not a taste of immortality but exactly the opposite. That which is wholly self-identical has no need to die.

The irony, however, is that death cannot be totalised either. One is always to some degree a stranger to one's death, unable to get a grip on it from the outside; and this is one of several respects in which it figures as a consummation of one's life, which similarly evades our grasp as an intelligible whole. 'Death', writes Slavoj Žižek, 'is precisely that which *cannot* be included into any totality. Its meaningless facticity is a permanent threat to meaning.'[14] Or as Quentin Meillassoux insists, death is the ultimate refutation of subjective idealism, since 'I think myself as mortal only if I think that my death has no need of my thought of death in order to be achieved'.[15] Rather as farce reduces human action to mere physical motion, so a corpse is a parcel of flesh from which meaning has haemorrhaged away, leaving it an inert lump of matter. It is no longer capable of generating sense, even though it may hold the most momentous significance for others.

Death draws a line under one's life, but it does not thereby invest it with a determinate direction, central meaning or aesthetically gratifying shape, so that one's existence continues to seem unbounded and death, in consequence, is bound to appear notional. One's death is both an absolute certainty and the very prototype of pure abstract speculation, like an ominous rumour picked up at second or third hand – unsettling but remote enough to shelve at present and attend to later. How can one experience as real an event which undercuts the reality of experience? Thomas Aquinas thought that the mind was incapable of seizing upon the concept of Creation because it was unable to grasp the notion of nothingness, nothingness being the only background against which the Creation as such might swim into view. If one's existence is similarly hard to get in one's sights, it is partly because, death being no more than a speculative affair, one really has nothing definitive from which to mark it off. And if the end of life can loom up as unreal, so can life itself when contemplated in the light of that cutting off. Anything that can vanish so irretrievably at any moment, however apparently substantial, is bound to have a smack of illusion about it, like a stage performance the very flamboyance of which (the sumptuous costumes, the glare of the lights, the larger-than-life gestures) seems designed to disavow the fact that it will imminently disappear.

Politics, so Thomas Hobbes considered, has much to do with death. To safeguard individuals from mortal injury at each other's hands is one of the primary functions of the political state. For Kant, it is epistemology rather than politics that bears witness to our mortal state, since finite animals like ourselves are for ever shut out from that synoptic view of the world and the self that we imagine is available to God, making do instead with this or that partial perspective on reality. It is God who has access to the noumenal realm, and can thus see us in the round, while it is a mark of our creatureliness, and thus of our mortality, that we ourselves do not. That human lives are untotalisable is why in the Christian view judgement can only ever be the Last Judgement, since only then, when the sprawling text of a life assumes the status of a closed book, is there a complete narrative to be assessed.

One can, to be sure, seek to convert one's existence into a totality of sorts by living in perpetual anticipation of one's death, a strategy advocated by both St Paul and Martin Heidegger.[16] In his *Religion within the Limits of Reason Alone*, Kant speaks of death as marking 'the necessity of standing ready at all times for the end',[17] while

Walter Benjamin sees every instant of time as the strait gate through which the Messiah might enter. If this is so, then one must live in a kind of tensed expectancy, lifting one's actions out of secular time and referring them forward to Judgement Day. Benjamin speaks in *The Origin of German Tragic Drama* of the tragic hero as one whose existence 'unfolds from death, which is not, to be sure, its end but its form.'[18] Perhaps to pre-empt or second-guess one's death in this way, converting it from the end point of one's existence to its inner dynamic, is the nearest one might come to experiencing it. In Benjamin's eyes, the enemy of this revolutionary, back-to-front conception of history is historicism, which holds that everything in the past can be stored and preserved in the form of cultural treasures and that nothing in the stately march of history can ever be definitively lost. It thus constitutes a denial of death on a collective scale. Georges Bataille speculates in an essay entitled 'Hegel, Death and Sacrifice' that sacrificing an animal in place of oneself may be a way of being present at one's own end. The Irish philosopher William Desmond claims that 'tragic insight crosses over from life to death and looks back on life, crosses back and lives life otherwise.'[19] One must, so to speak, live backwards from the grave.

T.S. Eliot writes in *Four Quartets* that it is the action on which one is intent at the time of death that will bear fruit in the lives of others. Yet since, as he adds, the moment of death is every moment – not only because a human heart can cease to thud at any second, but because we must be permanently prepared to encounter our end – it follows that this must be the case at any point of one's life. The most flourishing acts are those performed as though they were one's last, and thus accomplished not for their consequences but for their own sake. It is against utility or instrumental reason that this ethics of the graveyard sets its face, in contrast to the terrorist who destroys himself in order to maim and murder others. This is why Eliot urges us in the same breath not to think of the fruits of action. What will prove fertile for the future are acts that do not particularly keep it in mind. To be released by the contemplation of death from too narrow an investment in utility is to be free to live like the lilies of the field, treating one's existence and that of others as an end in itself. It is in this sense that living-towards-death and abundance of life are closely allied. The thought of death brings with it a certain invigorating recklessness, not least in our dealings with others, which is not to be mistaken for some swaggering insouciance.

Because we will not live to see the effects of our final actions, their fruitfulness is bound up with their selflessness, as with a martyr who will not live to witness the benefits he or she brings to others. An expenditure which anticipates no return is the most profusely rewarded. Our acts are prised loose from the tangled chains of causality and laid up beyond the ravages of time. It is for this reason that actions performed for their own sake have a peculiarly strong stink of mortality about them. In their cavalier carelessness of historical repercussions, they seem to point directly to eternity, and thus to death. For Jacques Derrida, there is a sense in which every ethical act brings us into death's presence, since our mortality marks the extreme limit of our vulnerability, and it is this fragility which speaks to us in the ethical demand. Only by being faithful to this demand until death, should this prove necessary, is a deed for Derrida truly ethical.[20] Perhaps this is to make too much of death, rather as Heidegger's emphasis falls on its momentousness but not on its everydayness. There is a sense in which the banality of death is as much a scandal as its crazed excessiveness.

One reason why we fear death is because it seems to nullify all that we have been. Why bother to brush one's teeth or set up as a small arms manufacturer when one will end up as a handful of dust? We are natural-born teleologists, for whom whatever cannot be laid up in eternity is likely to seem unbearably flimsy. It is hard to accept that what we do and feel has whatever value it has even though it will pass into oblivion. Hence the attitude of the protagonist of Woody Allen's film *Annie Hall*, who as a schoolboy refused to do his homework on the grounds that the universe is expanding and will one day break up entirely. (Thomas Nagel, however, points out that if what we do today will be irrelevant in a million years' time, the reverse must also be true, in which case the schoolboy's devious protest rests on dubious foundations. In any case, Nagel argues, to claim that something will not matter a million years hence has a point only if it matters now.)[21] Samuel Scheffler adopts a rather less apocalyptic version of this view in *Death and the Afterlife*, arguing that the assumption that the human race will survive our personal death, at least for a reasonable period of time, is vital to our current sense of value.

It may well be the case that the stock exchange, along with cancer research, mortgage applications and beginners' lessons in Ancient Greek, would collapse were we to know that the world was about to end, but Scheffler pays too little heed to the positive aspects of such a catastrophe. The historical document which most famously claims that the world is fast approaching its finale is the New Testament, but in its view the ethical implications of this belief are very different from having the stuffing knocked out of one's sense of value. On the contrary, viewing the world in the light of Judgement Day is what allows true value to become manifest. Since there is no time to engage in property deals or the marriage market, to decimate the rainforests or invade other nations' territories, all that matters is friendship and righteousness. The vision of the end of history liberates the self from the tyranny of temporality. 'Pure' value – value in itself – is what stands free of consequence and circumstance, as in the slogan 'Let justice be done though the world should perish'. In its unwavering resoluteness, this way of life belongs to an ethics of the Real. The moral imperative implicit in this view is not 'Act always with an eye to posterity', but 'Act always as if you and history were about to be annihilated'. In this respect, for the Christian Gospel as for William Blake, eternity is in some obscure sense here and now, concealed in the unfathomable depths of the present, in contrast to the conventional misconception (one common to Williams, Nagel and Scheffler) that what is at stake for religious faith is 'survival' or a limitless 'afterlife'. Eternity, as we have seen, is not to be confused with perpetuity. The central Christian event is not survival but resurrection – a radical transformation at odds with the consoling continuity of 'living on'.

To act in fine disregard of an aftermath is to fold the end of time back into the present, and thus to create an abbreviated image of eternity. One thinks of the cowardly Hirsch of Joseph Conrad's *Nostromo*, who to the reader's astonishment suddenly spits in the face of his executioner in the knowledge that for him there will be no consequences of this act beyond an instant bullet in the brain. Those who make their deaths their own have faced down the worst of horrors, and thus enjoy a rare degree of freedom. The Jew who refuses to kill a fellow Jew when commanded to do so by the Nazis, and who is therefore beaten to death himself, is no doubt aware that nothing will come of his action – that his colleague will be murdered in any case, and that the genocide will roll on unabated. This is not to say, however, that he dies in some gratuitous act of defiance. Rather, he dies to affirm the truth that love and pity have not vanished from the world, and that the true catastrophe would be when such terms were no longer even intelligible. He also dies in order to claim his death as his own, retrieving it as a free act from the forces that would enslave him. 'Our death', writes Maurice Blanchot of an end to life freely chosen, 'becomes the moment when we are most ourselves.'[22]

On this view, one which sets its face against all historicist or evolutionist thought, one should strive to treat every moment as absolute, disentangling it from the ignominy of circumstance, standing inside and outside of history at the same time by living from the end-times rather than simply in them. Jean-Joseph Goux speaks of Oedipus's initiation into death as lasting for almost a life-time, suspended as he is between living and dying:

> It is no longer a single event; it is a passage that is never completed, that must always be resumed and prolonged. It is the threshold situation (the liminal moment) that pervades all of life, that becomes the lived condition of an entire existence. The human condition in its entirety as a liminal state: this is how we might sum up the new ethics which emerges with Oedipus.[23]

No doubt this is what Paul has in mind when he speaks of us dying every moment, and what the Gospel means when it has Jesus refer to his death as his baptism. 'The only philosophy that can be responsibly practised', remarks Theodor Adorno, 'is the attempt to contemplate all things as they would present themselves from the standpoint of redemption.'[24]

All human acts have an aura of deathliness about them, since for good or ill they cannot be undone. This is one of the rare ways in which the absoluteness of death finds an echo in everyday life. Otherwise, death is too drastic a deprivation for the *Lebenswelt* to accommodate. We are not accustomed in everyday life to such startling transfigurations as being borne shoulder-high into a chapel to the sound of an organ. Whatever magnificent achievements we are able to chalk up when alive, none can equal the sheer drama of disappearing for ever and ever. Death is one of the few residues of the absolute in a secular age, and as such is at odds with its prevailing orthodoxies. Not to exist at all is far too surreal and extreme a state of affairs for the hard-nosed pragmatists who currently govern the globe, which is one reason why the prospect is so commonly disavowed. Only societies which maintain some notion of sacrifice, and thus some sense of death as the condition of life, are able to lift this repression. There is a sense in which it is not normal to be dead, as though not to be around at all is to commit some unspeakable solecism. Death is the ruin of meaning, sheer brute facticity, yet at the same time too earth-shaking an affair for us not to feel that it must harbour some portentous significance. If there is no death in the world of Samuel Beckett, simply a steady process of disintegration, it is because it would prove too brutally definitive an event in such an aporetic universe, in which even the act of hanging oneself from a tree demands more resoluteness than one can muster. To abandon this or that object is no reliable guide to what it might be like to abandon everything, which is of a different order altogether. Perhaps the absolute nature of death is one reason why it has proved so alluring to artists, since it is the closest analogy we have to pure creation. To wipe something from existence seems scarcely less miraculous than to bring it into being.

Contemplating all things from the standpoint of redemption, one is bound to confess, is a mighty tall order. One might imagine that it could be left to the plucky band of stalwarts known as martyrs, were it not that, for Christianity at least, martyrdom is a condition to which everyone is in principle summoned. A certain extremism is thus commonplace. It is of the nature of class history that the pursuit of justice may lead you to a squalid death at the hands of the political state, whether on Calvary or in the secret prisons of the intelligence services. Like tragedy, martyrdom is a way of reaping sense from what is otherwise a mere fact of Nature, turning one's mortality into a kind of rhetoric. Indeed, death as such couples the run-of-the-mill with the momentous in this way. Ernst Bloch yokes these twin features of it together when he remarks that 'nothing is so strange and grim as the blow that fells everyone'.[25] Death is an entirely natural phenomenon which is rarely experienced as such, being at once unremarkable and inconceivable. The fact that everyone without exception must suffer this calamitous loss simply compounds its strangeness, as though one were to find King Lears and Antigones loitering on every street corner. 'People die', comments a J.M. Coetzee character, 'it's human nature, you can't stop them.' The inconceivable happens all the time. The most commonplace of moments secretes the most catastrophic of potentials, as the strait gate through which at any instant death might enter. There is a startling contrast between the quotidian nature of death in general and the distinctly non-quotidian nature of one's own.

Death exposes the mind-warping gap between the spiritual *quidditas* or uniqueness of a man or woman and his or her utter biological dispensability. As a matter of Nature, the event is inevitable; but the cultural form it assumes is not, and neither in general is the mode of its occurrence, which remains largely contingent. Like sexuality, which is similarly cusped between the domains of Nature and Culture, it is difficult to avoid either overrating or underplaying it. As far as underplaying it goes, Tacitus records that the emperor Tiberius, seeking to placate the Roman populace for the scandalously meagre obsequies he laid on for the death of Germanicus, reminded them that men are mortal and only the state is immortal.[26] In similar spirit, Claudius points out to Hamlet with scarcely suppressed exasperation that death is part of a natural cycle, and that too plaintive a protest against it can be morbidly self-indulgent. This is true enough, but Hamlet is also right to regard death as excessive and intolerable. Whether it has value is another question. The most celebrated speech in the history of theatre hesitates between a life without merit, in which one meekly endures one's afflictions, and a rather more heroic grappling with one's sorrows which will put an end to them, though only at the price of putting an end to oneself.

Death has an authority that is hard to dispute. In *The Death of the Heart*, Elizabeth Bowen observes of one of her characters that her dying put her in a strong position for the first time in her life. Like love, death searches out what is most singular about a person, poignantly highlighting their irreplaceability. If one wanted a benign form of essentialism, one might find it here. One of Plato's objections to tragedy is that by furnishing us with images of death it reminds us of our apartness, thus undermining political solidarity. For Hegel, death, like law, is a universal truth which nonetheless confronts us with our utter irreducibility as individual selves, at once levelling and individuating. Like the human body, it is both an external fatality and radically one's own, a mode of distinction but also a shared condition. If it is in one sense inalienably mine, it can also be as mass-produced as sausage meat. Primo Levi speaks of death in the Nazi concentration camps as a trifling, banal, bureaucratic affair, scarcely distinguishable from everyday life. In Henry James's story 'The Beast in the Jungle', the monstrous event of which the narrator has spent his life in dread, one closely bound up with death, turns out to be both the terrifying spring of the beast and a void, a bathetic non-event, a fatally muffed opportunity.

Like the Stoics, one can choose to highlight the humdrum nature of death, treating it in the manner of Seneca's *On Consolation to Marcia* not only as a fact to be accepted but as a power to be affirmed. Death on this estimate is squarely on the side of the dispossessed, emancipating slaves, springing lifers from their prison cells, releasing the anguished from their afflictions, replacing conflict with tranquillity and cancelling the inequalities between rich and poor. It would be hard to imagine a more potent revolutionary force. Far from being the ruin of hope, death in Seneca's eyes is the very image of it. It is true that those sprung from their cells or freed from their torment by death are not able to take pleasure in this enviable state of affairs, but the fact remains that Nature has considerately supplied us with the means (suicide) of putting an end to our sufferings at any moment. Where there's death, there's hope.

This is true in a different sense for Thomas Mann's Thomas Buddenbrook, who not long before he dies is granted a vision of death as a more ecstatic form of liberation than the sober Seneca would envisage:

> Death was a joy, so great, so deep that it could be dreamed of only in moments of revelation like the present. It was the return from an unspeakably painful wandering, the correction of a grave mistake, the loosening of chains, the opening of doors – it put right again a lamentable mischance.

Thomas's vision is moving and mysterious enough to command respect; yet as the rest of the passage makes clear, it involves a dubious species of dualism for which the true self is imprisoned in its earthly body, and will be released on death to become part of a universal soul, flourishing more vigorously than ever. For all the splendour of the revelation, it is hard not to see in it a disavowal of personal dissolution.

For the Stoics, there is an egalitarianism about mortality which W.B. Yeats, who speaks of death's 'discourtesy', found hard to stomach. There is a touch of the mob about its relentless levelling. Yeats's call for men and women to come 'proud-eyed and laughing to the tomb' is a typical piece of Ascendancy swagger, of a piece with the hair-raisingly blasphemous epitaph he pens for himself in 'Under Ben Bulben'. With magnificent hauteur, death is to be dismissed as beneath the dignity of the Anglo-Irish gentry. One deals with one's mortality by turning a cold eye upon it, rather as one deals with an insolent valet. One is not to rage against the dying of the light but to stare stonily through it. While Virginia Woolf is insisting on the need for a room of one's own, Rilke, another spiritual aristocrat of the Yeatsian breed, observes in *The Notebooks of Malte Laurids Brigge* that a death of one's own is becoming increasingly hard to come by. One must protest in the name of an authentic demise against the shop-soiled, off-the-peg variety of the event which modernity has on offer like so many reach-me-down goods. Even death has been hijacked by the rabble. 'Ignorance of death is destroying us', comments Charlie Citrine in Saul Bellow's *Humboldt's Gift*, a judgement that Rilke would no doubt have endorsed. What might sound like consolation to some – the fact that if I die, then so does everyone else – is for Rilke sheer petty-bourgeois impertinence.

Rilke thus fails to see that a certain anonymity is natural to death. Like its partner *eros*, *thanatos* is no respecter of persons. The sexual orgy in which bodies are interchangeable has something in common with the concentration camp; but it also shows up the inherent impersonality of desire, which, like the death drive, one carries at the core of one's being yet is implacably indifferent towards. In this sense, death is both intimate and alien – an inmost possibility of *Dasein*, in Heideggerian idiom, yet a blind spot at the centre of the self which it is impossible to bring into focus, and as such another name for subjectivity itself. Benjamin speaks of the destruction of the tragic hero as 'familiar, personal, and inherent in him', while seeing him at the same time as shrinking from it as from some outlandish power.[27] If the negativity of death is in some sense the consummation of subjectivity, then it follows that we only coincide with ourselves completely when it is no longer possible for us to do so.

Despite its bluster, Yeats's disdain for death has something to recommend it. From St Paul's 'where is thy sting?' to John Donne's 'Death, thou shalt die', there is an honourable tradition of deriding death, mocking its self-importance and cutting it satirically down to size. This is to repay it in its own coin, since it is a renowned debunker itself, and thus has affinities with comedy as well as tragedy. In the face of fervid convictions and vaulting ambitions, it insists that we all come to utter disaster. The Christian belief is that in tit-for-tat, handy-dandyish style, the Resurrection in turn brings death to nothing. Its intimidating power, like that of some ranting despot, is unmasked as bogus. No doubt there is something a touch too cavalier about Albert Camus's comment in *The Myth of Sisyphus* that there is no fate that cannot be surmounted by scorn; but it is true even so that wit, satire and mockery are resources to be stored against one's mortal ruin. Like the Law, death is an imperious, enigmatic, implacable power which threatens to reduce the human subject to so much dross, confronting it with the paltriness of its own existence and violently breaching its identity and autonomy. If the Law, along with the sin it unwittingly fosters, are for St Paul what brings death into the world, it is also an image of that mortality; and in the apostle's view the two are vanquished together in the crucifixion and resurrection of Jesus. The Resurrection is death not abolished but transformed, reinterpreted, refashioned and so objectively no longer to be feared – however much, like children terrified by a bogeyman they know to be an illusion, we persist in doing so.

Christianity may debunk death, but it also regards it as an abomination. It is abhorrent because it involves an irreparable loss, and thus confronts us with too little; but also because it exposes us to an intolerable *jouissance*, and thus to too much. St Paul has no doubt in his First Letter to the Corinthians that death is the enemy of humanity, one which is to be outflanked and defeated not by vigorous combat but by being boldly embraced. The theologian Herbert McCabe speaks bluntly of death as 'an outrage'.[28] There is no way in which we can prove equal to its crazed immoderateness. Like the Freudian superego, its demands are absurdly extreme. Like the superego, too, it lacks the good sense to recognise that we are scarcely capable of acceding to them.

For the Christian Gospel, death is to be accepted but not endorsed. The philosopher Gabriel Marcel speaks of a 'non-capitulating acceptance' of it. We should not allow its two-a-penny nature to blunt our sense of its importunity, like respectable citizens who turn an embarrassed blind eye to some piece of Dadaist lunacy in their midst. It is violent, excessive and unmannerly, tearing us from our loved ones and consigning our projects contemptuously to the dust. The fact that it is also natural – the way the species bears in upon the individual, as Marx comments – is no consolation. Typhoid is natural. If we ought freely to submit to death's indignity, it is not because there is anything in the least tolerable about it, but because to do so involves a form of self-giving, which is also the most estimable way to live.

The easiest way to die is to give way to that implacable negativity at the heart of the subject which Freud calls the death drive. It is not just that death then becomes a Dionysian delight or ecstatic dissolution, but that we are able to indulge to the full our corrosive hostility to life as such, our sullen rejection of its specious allure, venting all the rage of a frustrated infant turning furiously upon a parent who has been shown to have feet of clay. It is, however, a disgust that renders death too facile. It must therefore be worked upon if death is to become the sacrifice of something precious, and hence a source of value. To accept one's death is an act of humility. It is to recognise that one's existence is one signifier among many of the gratuitousness of all Being, and that it is not one's own to dispose of. To acknowledge one's dispensability is thus to recognise Being itself as it truly is, in an act of supreme realism which is no doubt in any full sense beyond our power.

*　*　*

In J.K. Rowling's *Harry Potter and the Deathly Hallows*, the protagonist is said to have 'accepted, even embraced, the possibility of death', and the same is true of Shakespeare's Claudio in *Measure for Measure*:

If I must die,

I will encounter darkness as a bride

And hug it in my arms. (Act III Scene 1)

In Heideggerian phrase, Claudio becomes free for (his own) death.[29] He is speaking, one should note, of how he will cope with his mortality if he is called upon to do so, not of some Hamlet-like hunger for oblivion. He differs in this respect from a lineage of tragic protagonists, from Sophocles' Antigone and Racine's Phèdre to the eponymous hero of Büchner's *Danton's Death*, Ibsen's Hedda Gabler and Hickey of Eugene O'Neill's *The Iceman Cometh*, who are all in one way or another in love with death. Claudio is not exactly a martyr, since he does not bequeath his death as a gift to others. Yet even when the martyr does not do so directly, he or she usually dies to protect a principle that is vital for the welfare of others. It is a more fruitful conjuncture of *eros* and *thanatos* than anything to be found in Freud. Even so, Claudio resembles a martyr in his reluctance to perish. 'I have hope to live, and am prepar'd to die', he informs the Duke. If he must meet his end, then in a delectably perverse interweaving of *eros* and *thanatos*, his death will be disarmed by being fiercely, tenderly loved. Rilke speaks in his fourth *Duino Elegy* of the mystery by which one can hold death 'to one's heart, gently, and not refuse to go on living'. In a triumph of *amor fati*, Claudio will rise above his demise by wooing it, winning it over to his side and thus defusing its terrors. To perform one's death actively is to snatch victory from the jaws of defeat, conjuring something out of nothing. It is to pluck a value from a fact by finding meaning in the end of meaning. As such, it is a microcosm of tragedy. Antony of *Antony and Cleopatra* echoes Claudio's words:

> But I will be
> A bridegroom in my death, and run towards it
> As to a lover's bed. (Act IV Scene 14)

Like Claudio, Antony is speaking of how he intends to die if he has to, not of any great eagerness to expire. He is no more of a martyr than Claudio, since he does not donate his death to others; but like the martyr he finds the truth of his being, in Lacanian phrase, in assuming the lack that he is. Unable to give up on his desire, he will invest it instead in his death, merging *eros* with *thanatos* and finding himself transported into some strange liminal zone between life and death, like all those possessed by the desire of the Real.[30] There is a tradition of such part-defiant, part-submissive, part-affirmative deaths in tragedy, from the incestuous Giovanni and Annabella of John Ford's *'Tis Pity She's a Whore* to the ecstatic self-dissolution of Wagner's Tristan and Isolde and the *Liebestod* of Johannes Rosmer and Rebekka West in Ibsen's *Rosmersholm*. (It is worth noting in this respect how much late literary art centres on the themes of death and redemption or resurrection, from Shakespeare, Milton and Goethe to Dickens, Wagner, Ibsen, Tolstoy, Joyce and T.S. Eliot.) Those who can live their deaths to the full seek to break the demonic compulsion of the death drive, taking their dying authoritatively in hand. Their aim is to convert necessity into a form of freedom. To accomplish this is to bear witness to the truth that there is something in the human subject which is more than itself – that Lacanian Thing or Cause which represents unconditional value, and for the sake of which these acolytes of the Real are prepared to sacrifice their very existence. It signifies that surplus or excess over itself which makes the subject what it is – a surplus for which God is one traditional name, but which goes under a range of other pseudonyms as well: honour for the Homeric heroes, chastity for Samuel Richardson's Clarissa, authenticity for the Sartrian protagonist, a reputable name among one's peers for Willy Loman and Eddie Carbone, the death drive for Jacques Lacan.

As far as one's stance to death goes, Claudio's opposite number in *Measure for Measure* is Barnardine, a death-row psychopath who refuses to make anything of his impending execution because he lives the kind of torpid, Bartleby-like existence that is already a kind of death. As such, he is the antithesis of Lampedusa's protagonist in

The Leopard, who 'had done his best to organise for himself as much of death as he could while actually going on living'. Like Giorgio Agamben's Muselmann, Barnardine is unable to make any sense of his death since the capacity for meaning has already deserted him. His apathy thus poses a subversive threat to the state. As long as he remains indifferent to his approaching end, power ceases to have a hold over him and thereby stands discredited. By dying to yourself as Barnardine does, turning yourself into an inert lump of matter before others have the chance to do it for you, you insolently pre-empt the authority of death and leave nothing of yourself to be negated. This spiritual sluggard, who enjoys what the Provost calls 'the liberty of the prison', must therefore be persuaded 'willingly to die'. Unless he somehow performs his death, making it his own, it will fail to count as an event in his life and will therefore be impervious to the signifi-cance with which the state seeks to invest it. As the demented anar-chist professor of Joseph Conrad's *The Secret Agent* boasts, 'I depend on death, which knows no restraint and cannot be attacked. My superiority is evident.'

Barnardine is in Giorgio Agamben's term a kind of Muselmann, suspended somewhere between life and death. In the case of the Muselmann of the concentration camps, this is the consequence of a trauma lacerating enough to extinguish subjectivity itself. The Muselmann is thus the victim who survives his own death, one whose identity has been broken beyond repair but who nonetheless lives on as a spectre of himself. For Christianity, the evil responsible for this condition can be overcome only by an equally deathly transformation – that undergone by the subject of baptism, which survives its own death (this time by symbolic drowning) in a sense

more affirmative than the derelict inmates of Auschwit
view, it is by the 'trauma' of a sacramental encounter with
and resurrection of Christ that one can survive one's own
converting it into a form of life or self-giving, one which p(
speaking stands at the opposite pole from the Nazi camps.

The martyr seeks to live his death in the here and now, se
as incarnate in the perishable stuff of the body rather than sim
a future event. Barnardine represents a grisly parody of this c
tion. Both he and Claudio embrace nothingness; yet there is a di
ence between the cynic's or nihilist's way of anticipating his end,
which, as with the play's streetwise Lucio, levels all values and stri
all odds even, and a prefiguring of it that puts all such value in ch:
tening perspective. If life foreshadows death by being a foretaste
its futility, there is no reason why relinquishing one's existenc
should prove a problem. This is one reason why Barnardine is not
afraid of death – unlike Claudio, who quakes at the very thought of
it. All the same, it is the fact that Claudio is fearful of his end that
lends his assent to it such value. Dying becomes a strenuous project
rather than a piece of moral indolence.

'Not to dislike the idea of dying', writes Montaigne, 'is truly
possible only in one who enjoys living.'[31] As a Stoic of sorts, he means
perhaps that truly to relish one's life involves a certain judicious inner
detachment which already foreshadows one's end. Genuine enjoyment must involve a certain consciousness of itself, as mindless
immersion does not. It is the mindlessly immersed who will find
death a terror, not those self-aware enough to keep one steady eye on
it in the midst of their pleasures. The martyr rejects the world out of
love for it, which is where he or she differs from the suicide. 'This

man loved earth, not heaven, enough to die', reads a line from a Wallace Stevens poem. The suicide discards a life that has become worthless, whereas the martyr yields up what he or she regards as precious. Otherwise it can be hard at first glance to tell the difference between the two. When St John speaks of spurning the world, he means rejecting the malign principalities and powers that did Jesus to death, not rejecting material Creation as such, which is blessed because it is God's handiwork. Hence John's comment that God's passion for the world is such that he sent his only son to redeem it.

St Paul writes in Ephesians of 'our struggle [being] not against flesh and blood, but against leaders, authorities, against the world rulers of this darkness'. It is not the body or the material realm that the martyr repudiates, but an oppressive power structure. One must be well disposed to worldly things, but not to the point where one is so comfortably reconciled to reality as to let the ruling powers off the hook and excuse their murderous conduct. For Jacques Lacan, following in the footsteps of Descartes and Hegel, a primordial, purely negative, quasi-psychotic gesture of withdrawal from the world is necessary – not as an end in itself, but as the essential condition of any significant engagement with it. This, in effect, is the situation of the martyr. It is also the condition of baptism, in which the world in the pejorative sense of the word is renounced as the subject is symbolically drowned, invested with a new identity and ushered into a symbolic order (the Christian community) bound together by love rather than power.

Martyrdom is not a destiny to be sought out. 'There's always the ultimate self-deception', comments a character in P.D. James's *Devices and Desires*, 'the final arrogance. Martyrdom.' Those who clamour to

be burnt at the stake are not saints but reckless adventurists in hot pursuit of celestial bounty. There were, to be sure, hordes of early Christians alarmingly keen to divest themselves of their mortality, stridently demanding to be thrown to the lions or put to the sword.[32] Some of them deliberately provoked the exasperated authorities into arresting them. A number of Donatist heretics, avid for divine glory, would offer themselves up for slaughter to any armed travellers they happened to encounter, even threatening to kill them if they did not comply. 'It was their daily spirit to kill themselves', writes St Augustine, 'by throwing themselves off cliffs, or into the water, or into the fire.'[33] Aspiring martyrs with a canny eye on their eternal reward (Islamist suicide bombers, for example) fail to learn the lesson of Thomas Becket in Eliot's *Murder in the Cathedral*, who warns of the dangers of doing the right thing for the wrong reason, embracing one's death for the sake of heavenly recompense. The point, as in *Four Quartets*, is not to think of the fruits of action, for fear of adopting the instrumental rationality of those against whom your action is aimed. The problem is how to do so without also denying responsibility for the consequences of what you do, as well as without falling prey to a spuriously existentialist cult of action for its own sake.

Thomas's bowing to death will indeed bear fruit, but only if he performs it without a close consideration of its effects. Similarly, if Jesus had regarded his hour on Calvary simply as a passage to eternal glory, he would not have been raised from the dead. Only by living one's death to the full can it be converted from a cul-de-sac to a horizon. The Resurrection does not annul the tragedy of the Crucifixion, the livid marks of which Jesus's risen body still bears.

The true martyr is the one who is prepared to let everything go, even the hope of salvation. Martin Luther was of this persuasion. So is Rupert Birkin in D.H. Lawrence's *Women in Love*, whose radical self-dissolution would betray itself were he to imagine a more tolerable future. In this sense, the martyr acts out the condition of utter self-dispossession to which all men and women will anyway be reduced, plucking a virtue from necessity.

The Donatist heretics are a far cry from Martin Luther King Jr, who in his last public speech put in a good word for longevity while appearing to foresee his own assassination. They are also a far cry from Gethsemane, a scene interpolated by the Gospel writers to demonstrate among other things that Jesus has no desire to die. Instead, he is portrayed as convulsed by panic and terror at the thought of his impending execution. You do not qualify as a martyr unless you cherish your life. There is no merit in casting off what you find pointless in any case. Giving up drinking bleach for Lent is not generally considered a sacrifice. 'She likes giving up', remarks Celia Brooke of her sister Dorothea in George Eliot's *Middlemarch*, to which Dorothea responds, 'If that were true, Celia, my giving up would be self-indulgence, not self-mortification.' History is easy enough to abjure if, like Schopenhauer or Lacan, you regard it as a cesspit in the first place. Jean-Luc Marion writes of the specious form of sacrifice in which you give up features of the self not thought to be essential to it in any case.[34] Yeats's great poem 'Sailing to Byzantium' celebrates the sensual delights of the very profane sphere on which it turns its back. It is more than can be said for T.S. Eliot's 'Ash Wednesday' or *Four Quartets*, poems which grant the secular such a paltry value that the price of repudiating it is hardly exorbitant. The

New Testament, by contrast, teaches that to live well is to live abundantly, but at the same time requires its disciples to lay down their lives should the occasion arise. If this is an arduous demand, it is not just because death is fearful but because an abundant life is not an easy one to abdicate.

To have nothing worth abnegating one's life for, one might claim, is to be poor indeed. For the martyr, life is so sweet that even death must be pressed into its service, *thanatos* harnessed to the ends of *eros*. She is obliged to forfeit her existence for the sake of what makes life worth living. This is why it is hard to say whether she goes to her death willingly or not. If it is a free decision, it is also one forced upon her by unpalatable circumstance, like someone who leaps from a high building to escape a raging fire. It is not exactly that the martyr chooses to die, but that he chooses to defend a principle to the death, or opts for a form of life that makes his execution more or less inevitable. In doing so, he typically converts the act of dying into a public theatre. Richardson's Clarissa, who dedicates herself to death in a solemn, public, elaborately protracted ceremony, is exemplary, even hyperbolic in this respect. As David Wood puts it, 'To be a sacrifice is to transform one's individual life into something whose significance transcends that individuality.'[35]

Robin Young speaks of martyrs as being 'like letters meant to be read by the community and the world.'[36] To be martyred is to allow one's death to be taken into public ownership, undergoing a form of semiosis in which one's body is converted into a sign. The act of dying becomes an eloquent piece of discourse, as the flesh speaks more persuasively than any voice. 'In the presence of the suffering [tragic] hero', writes Walter Benjamin, 'the community learns reverence and gratitude for the word with which his death endowed it.'[37] Like the lover, the martyr offers others not gifts or tokens but his or her own body, which like the widow's mite is the most sumptuous form of self-giving. 'The sacrificer', comment Henri Hubert and Marcel Mauss, 'gives up something of himself but he does not give himself. Prudently, he sets himself aside.'[38] No such reserve marks the lover or martyr, for whom sign and referent, gift and giver, are at one, and who – as John Milbank remarks of the gift – represents 'the exact point of intersection between the real and the signifying'.[39]

The tragedy of the martyr is not simply that she dies, but that her death should be required in the first place. Martyrdom testifies to the need to change the conditions that make it essential. If it is appalling, it is not least (to paraphrase Bertolt Brecht on tragedy) because it ought to be unnecessary. There would be no call for such figures in a just society. Offering one's body to be burnt is an image not of the good life, but of what it might take to achieve it. Conviviality is a deeper ethic than self-denial, and the latter makes sense only in terms of the former.[40] If the austerely self-sacrificial virtues have their place, it is because justice and well-being are not possible without them. In a corrupt world, remarks John Milbank, 'the only way to the recovery of mutual interaction will pass through sacrifice to death'.[41]

That this is so is itself a tragic affair. The Eucharist is a utopian image of a festive future, but also a sharing in the self-destitution necessary for its arrival. In dying to one world, the martyr bears witness to the possibility of another, and the implacable absolute-ness of his or her death marks the discontinuity between the two. As both victim of the old and harbinger of the new, she is the sign of a revolutionary *transitus* between the two orders, as is Walter Benjamin's tragic protagonist in *The Origin of German Tragic Drama*. Yet there is no guarantee that this transition will be safely accomplished. There can be no unequivocal underwriting of it by the Other, which is why it involves a supreme act of faith – a giving of oneself, as Jean-Luc Marion puts it, without knowing in advance whether one is saving or losing oneself.[42] Only against the background of one's mortality will the Cause or Thing to which one is pledged stand out in all its luminous depth. But the Kantian purity of the act is always likely to be stained by 'pathological' motives – malice, vainglory, masochism, intransigence, morbidity, narcissism, self-loathing, visceral aggression, the obscene gratifications of the death drive. Most of these qualities can be detected in Clarissa Harlowe's astonishingly theatrical death. Eliot's Becket cannot be certain that a lust for fame is not to be counted among his motives. Is Milly Theale's gesture of forgiveness at the end of Henry James's novel *The Wings of the Dove* the highest ethical act or the last word in devious manipulation? Is James's heroine beautifully disinterested or a scheming avenger? We shall be looking into this question later.

Martyrdom, no doubt, has its obscene underside. Selfless dedication is never far from the erotic spasms of the death drive. Plato speaks in the *Phaedo* of philosophy as a meditation on death, and as such a disentanglement from lowly corporeal pleasures; but this overlooks the carnal delights of the death drive. As with most other human activities, there must be something in martyrdom for the agent himself, even if it is no more than the satisfaction of knowing that he is doing the right thing. 'There is one case of sacrifice', comment Hubert and Mauss, 'in which selfish calculation is absent.

This is the case of the sacrifice of the god, for the god who sacrifices himself gives himself irrevocably.'[43] This is not, however, a gesture available to mere humanity. To give oneself whole and entire in the manner of the martyr or the lover may be a less ambiguous affair than to offer oneself in gift or speech, but it does not, for all that, escape the duplicitous mark of the signifier. 'Charity, as if it didn't have enough problems in this day and age', remarks Saul Bellow's Herzog, 'will always be suspected of morbidity – sado-masochism, perversity of some sort. All higher or moral tendencies lie under suspicion of being rackets.' It is certainly true of Thomas Hobbes, the greatest of English political philosophers, who can see nothing in the act of giving but a ploy to secure the service or friendship of another, gain a reputation for charity or magnanimity, deliver oneself from the discomforts of compassion or seal one's reward in heaven. For Hobbes, no rational creature gives without a steely eye to his or her own advantage.[44] Neither is there any assurance that one's gift of death will not be travestied, rebuffed or misread. Not being able to know exactly what one is about when performing such acts is part of the riskiness of the situation.

*   *   *

To live in anticipation of death is not necessarily to live abstemiously. The Christian faith contrasts in this respect with the ascetic vision of Alain Badiou, for whom ethics can have no truck with anything as distastefully mundane as pleasure, virtue, interests, happiness or self-realisation.[45] There is a similar ascetic quality to the thought of Jacques Lacan, a former Roman Catholic whose brother was a Benedictine monk. Desire in Lacan's judgement is not of this world.

Indeed, Lacan regards Kant's august moral law as desire in its purest state, sacrificing all particular objects and interests to some impossible *jouissance* on the far side of the pleasure principle. Desire is the modern version of transcendence. God has been ousted by the unending search for him. This form of desire, Lacan remarks, 'culminates in the sacrifice, strictly speaking, of everything that is the object of love in one's human tenderness – I would say, not only in the rejection of the pathological object, but in its sacrifice and murder.'[46] In this sense, desire lies on the side of death and annihilation, not pleasure and fulfilment. Conversely, there is a sense in which the death drive, striving to defeat the flow of temporality with its compulsive repetitions, represents a way of being undead, and so lies on the side of the living.

The poverty practised by the monastic orders, however, reflects no animus against material things. It is a way of prefiguring one's end, when one will be stripped of one's selfhood as well as one's worldly goods, and hence of testifying to the transience of the present. To bear witness to the passing away of what some fondly regard as imperishable is among other things to proclaim the feebleness of the powers of this world. There is a Jewish mystical tradition for which to divest oneself of material attachments is a kind of proleptic death.[47] The ashes worn by the faithful on their foreheads on Ash Wednesday are a satirical comment on those who behave as though they will live for ever: celebrities, millionaire bankers, crooked presidents and the like. Such men and women are true subjects of the unconscious, which in Freud's view knows no mortality and cannot represent death. Those who can rehearse their ultimate self-dispossession along the way no doubt stand a better chance of settling their accounts with death than the well heeled, whose privilege and prosperity make it harder for them to die. This is why the New Testament harbours such grim forebodings about their celestial prospects. It is also one reason why it is so implacably ill-disposed to the family, an institution which tends to bind men and women to the status quo. Like William Golding's Pincher Martin, those who are bound fast to this world by power or wealth may find themselves confronting death by clinging to themselves for dear life, unable to trust that were they simply to let go they would meet with no worse fate than slipping gently into oblivion.

Monks and nuns are celibate for something like the reason that guerrilla fighters may need to be. They are eunuchs for the kingdom, whose mission would simply be hampered by property and pregnancy, and whose forgoing of a single intimate relationship makes them more available for the love and care of others. What is at stake is not an aversion to sexuality or material goods but a provisional suspension of them in the name of a cause even more precious. For St Paul, it is sexual love, not celibacy, that is a sign of the coming kingdom. Excess, not austerity, is a foretaste of the future. Heaven is a matter of lavish banqueting, not mortifying the flesh. It is simply that marriage and domesticity are scarcely the most suitable lifestyles for those who labour for that goal, any more than they are for the professional revolutionary. All relationships and commitments must be rethought in the light of the imminent end of history. The problem is one of how to re-evaluate all values in the light of mortality without thereby repudiating them as so much dross in the manner of the cynic or nihilist. St Paul speaks in his First Letter to the Corinthians of 'those who deal with the world as though they had no dealings with the world', which is not to be mistaken for some lordly *apatheia*. To engage with the world while refusing to absolutise it is as much a mark of the political militant as it is of the monk.

The revolutionary, with his Spartan self-discipline, is no image of the order he is out to construct. As Bertolt Brecht's poem 'To Those Born in Later Times' remarks, those who seek to lay the ground for friendship cannot themselves be friendly. The monk or nun, similarly, is no positive sign of the eschatological future. Poverty, celibacy and obedience will not be features of the coming dispensation. Instead, the monk renounces worldly goods in order to testify to their impermanence, and thus to a power that transcends the present. If such acts of renunciation are to be a question of sacrifice, it follows that the monk or nun must hold the goods he or she forgoes (freedom, sexuality, material possessions and the like) in high regard, and that the future for which they are forsworn must therefore be even more estimable. In their strategic refusal of the pleasures of the present, such figures convert themselves into a negative sign of the future, whose fulfilments will beggar what we can experience now. They might be said to act out in ethical terms the very condition of subjectivity itself, the subject being that (non-)entity which is constituted as such only through loss. To pluck something positive from this negativity is to convert a fact into a value. Paul's insistence that we die every moment is both biologically valid (since time means decay) and phenomenologically true (since subjectivity is a continually self-negating project); yet it is also a moral imperative, one which requires that we turn this given feature of the human condition to transformative ends. It asks us to convert necessity into free decision.

Not all self-giving is of a sacrificial sort. Sacrifice is the kind of self-giving that hurts. The more fulfilling form of it is love, in which the self is enriched by being bestowed, augmented by being yielded up; but at the same time it involves the pain and anxiety of risk, along with a high degree of vulnerability. Love is a foretaste of the loss of the self in death, which is why to live in anticipation of that end is the reverse of living abstemiously. Only those well schooled in relinquishing themselves are truly capable of dying, yet to live this way is also to flourish. In this sense, death constitutes the inner structure of the good life. It is here that *eros* and *thanatos* are most closely interwoven, and it is on the act of martyrdom above all that they converge.

Caritas or *agape*, however, would be more appropriate terms here than *eros*. It is because the love at stake here is the properly impersonal business of charity that it need not prove inimical to an acceptance of death, which shares its anonymity. 'Love is not a feeling', Ludwig Wittgenstein once wrote, meaning that a sensation that lasted only ten seconds could be pain but not love. The same is true, however, if one thinks of love as *caritas* rather than the erotic or romantic variety. One is not required to feel tender sentiments towards those one rescues from white slave traffickers or sherry party bores. This is why the paradigm of love for the New Testament is love of strangers and enemies rather than of friends. Charity is a social practice, not a state of mind. One is expected to take another's place in the queue for the gas chambers, but whether the two of you are on intimate terms is neither here nor there. Because *eros* is a matter of sentiment, however, it binds us more intimately to others and thus makes dying a more arduous affair. This is not so true of *caritas*.

It is this connection between two kinds of death, one literal and one metaphorical, that the Heidegger of *Being and Time* conspicuously fails to forge. Being-towards-death and being-with-others are both constitutive structures of *Dasein*, but their affinity goes largely unexamined. It is being with others, not for them, that claims the philosopher's attention, and even then more cursorily than *Dasein's* other dimensions. One must appropriate one's death, but not in order to offer it as a gift to others. Self-giving for the later Heidegger is largely a question of the children of the Fatherland stretching themselves obediently on its sacrificial altar. Indeed, individual authenticity is finally at odds with being-with-others. Faced with the imminence of death (and the imminence of death is every moment), *Dasein* finds itself thrown back in a stark moment of solitude on its own possibilities, such that 'all relations to other *Dasein* are dissolved in it'.[48] '*Dasein's* experience of its ownmost [*sic*] possibility', comments Giorgio Agamben in *Language and Death*, 'coincides with its experience of the most extreme negativity'.[49] The meaning of life is death, though not quite in the sense that Freud or St Paul had in mind.

To anticipate one's death involves confronting what Heidegger calls 'one's own most non-relational possibility of being', so that 'the non-relational character of death ... individualises *Dasein* down to itself'.[50] Death, he observes, '*is* always just one's own', which was not the view of the poet John Donne.[51] If death is so definitive of *Dasein*, it is because it lays bare the indissoluble core that shows the self up as non-relational. It is one's irreplaceability that is illuminated by one's mortality. In Lacanian idiom, the Real is that starkly irreducible singularity at the core of the human subject, excessive of all cultural features and contingent qualities, which is where we are both most solitary and most universal, and of which death is the primary signifier. The only form of relationship that will prove durable is one which can accommodate this radical non-relationality – which is to say that all valid relationships in some sense involve a relation to death, encountering the other at his or her most needy and desolate. It is this state of destitution that must be shared. For Heidegger, by contrast, death is not to be seen as a self-dispossession akin to the condition of being-with-others.[52] It is not an event to be shared, as the Christian Eucharist is a communion in death. 'Non-existence is not for sharing', remarks Jean-Luc Nancy,[53] but there is a sense in which this is precisely true of martyrdom. It is also true of the tragedies of Oedipus and Lear, in which only an acknowledgement of nothingness can provide the social order with a foundation robust enough to build on.

For Heidegger, appropriating one's death is a heroic affair. It is the prerogative of the spiritually patrician few, not a condition of which *das Man* – his contemptuous term for the deluded masses – is remotely capable. Those who were exterminated in the Nazi camps were also, in Heidegger's view, incapable of such an act. For *Dasein* to anticipate its own end is for it to become conscious of its 'lostness in the they-self', and in rising above this degenerate state shake itself free from the false consciousness of the rabble. As Simon Critchley remarks of the Heideggerian tragic hero, 'it is only by opposing the inauthentic historical ground of the polis that *Dasein* can become authentically historical'.[54] There are those who merely meet their biological end, and then there is a privileged elite who are able to reap supreme value from their own demise. Tragedy is what sorts the great of soul from the poor in spirit. Death is a question of individual authenticity, not the logical consummation of a selfless devotion to others. For *Being and Time*, the non-being that matters is not what the Hebrew Bible names the *anawim* or scum of the earth, the living dead from a compact with whom all authentic existence flows. What matters is *my* death, which no one can perform in my place. In austerely Protestant spirit, each of us shoulders the solitary burden of his guilt and salvation. Life is a matter between myself and death, rather than death being a matter between myself and others. There is no sense in which death and dispossession might lay the groundwork of a new form of *Mitsein*.

* * *

One might claim that the death of Jesus undermines Heidegger's contrast between an authentic and an inauthentic end, as a member of the rabble makes his death his own in the name of all those ignoble wretches for whose mode of meeting their fate Heidegger shows little but contempt. Tragedy and heroism are hard to distinguish in *Being and Time*, whereas the New Testament, intriguingly, is a tragic document but not a heroic one. G.E. Lessing comments in his *Dramatic Notes* that the character of a true Christian is quite untheatrical. The locus of the Gospel is everyday life. Indeed, Charles Taylor has attributed the very concept of the quotidian to Christianity.[55] Its protagonist is an obscure, low-life itinerant who suffers a humiliating defeat at the hands of imperial power. In what can only be seen as either a moral obscenity or an exceedingly sick joke, the Messiah himself is flayed and butchered. His carnivalesque entry into the metropolitan capital constitutes a satirical comment on the mystique of kingship. The Gospel proclaims the vaingloriousness of all worldly power, the wreckage of all grandiose spiritual schemes and bright-eyed political panaceas. Only a solidarity with non-being, pressed if necessary to the point of death, can confound the principalities of this world. In contrast to Heidegger's noble-spirited coterie, all are called to be baptised into this squalid action, and thus summoned to potential martyrdom. If necessary, they must give up their material goods, abandon their family and friends and lead a hand-to-mouth existence in a cause that might steer them to torture and execution at the hands of the state. Jesus makes it brutally plain to his comrades that if they are true to his mission they are likely to encounter much the same end as himself. It is an absurdly extremist doctrine. Of all the excellent reasons for not being a Christian, this – along with the fact that if God exists, he must be hopelessly in love with Donald Trump – is surely the most persuasive.

For the Gospel, being steadfast for death thus involves a specific form of life, not some morbid necrophilia or otherworldly rapture. The twentieth century was to witness an unsavoury liaison between the ideas of death, will, self-sacrifice, authenticity, spiritual aristoc-racy and the spurning of the commonplace, a syndrome in which Heidegger himself played his disreputable part. It is not always easy to distinguish the recklessness this cult involves from a more precious kind of prodigality. Thom Gunn's poem 'Lerici' is a case in point. It is a superbly accomplished piece, in Gunn's taut, tightly disciplined early style; but the lean, laconic form reflects a certain subdued swagger in the content, as the poem contrasts the supposedly submissive end of the epicene Shelley, falling 'submissive through the waves', for whom the darkness of death is like a consoling nurse, with those more virile types who 'make gestures with arms open wide' and embrace it like a bride. These men compress into the moment of death all the energies they would have expended had they continued to live. Death here is not accepted but faced down, in a mixture of Nietzschean haughtiness, Yeatsian defiance and tough-minded existentialist rebellion – a generous refusal to calculate borders on a celebration of violence and a glorification of death: 'Strong swimmers, fishermen, explorers: such / Dignify death by fruitless violence, / Squandering all their little left to spend'. The poem exudes a desperate, foolhardy vein of heroism. Giving over and above the measure is less largesse of spirit than a mocking imitation of death's own gratuitousness, miming its futility rather than bowing to its authority. Mimesis – the human imitation of Nature – is a well-worn device for achieving dominion over natural forces. By acting out the profligacy of death, satirically outdoing its own exorbitance, one can achieve a bleak Pyrrhic victory over its implacable power. If death is a bride, however, it is one to be mastered rather than, as with Shakespeare's Claudio, gathered tenderly in one's arms. Gunn's 'arms open wide' suggests less an erotic embrace than a vauntingly virile gesture. This is a poem about *jouissance* – about the devil-may-care exuberance or obscene gratification which flows from the prospect of annihilation.[56]

A different kind of profligacy is advocated by the New Testament. Jacques Derrida remarks in *The Gift of Death*, speaking of Abraham's readiness to sacrifice Isaac, that what he offers 'is given back to him because he renounced calculation'.[57] The moral economy presented in the Gospel, Derrida insists, 'breaks with exchange, symmetry, or reciprocity', a claim which overlooks the fact that comradeship and communality lie at the core of its teaching.[58] It is true, however, that such reciprocity is not necessarily at odds with a magnificent refusal to reckon the cost. An *acte gratuit* can always be shared. In Shakespeare's *Antony and Cleopatra*, Antony's claim that 'there's beggary in the love that can be reckon'd', which is meant to describe the bond between him and Cleopatra, suggests that reckless profusion can be as much a matter of mutual as of unilateral giving. Thomas Hardy writes in *Far from the Madding Crowd* of erotic love as involving 'a sense of exorbitant profit, spiritually by an exchange of hearts', thus combining excess and mutuality.

Even so, Derrida is right to discern what he calls an 'absolute surplus value' in the Christian idea of *caritas*, since there may be no great virtue in loving those who love you in return. Reciprocity in this sense of the term may certainly be suspect. As Matthew's Gospel points out, there is no distinction in saluting your brethren only. Luke counsels against inviting to your feasts only those who might invite you to their dinner table in return. 'There is an economy', Derrida remarks of the New Testament, 'but it is an economy that integrates the renunciation of a calculable remuneration.'[59] One is expected to turn the other cheek, return good for evil, bless those who revile you, give away one's cloak as well as one's coat, walk two miles rather than one, forgive seventy times seven. These spendthrift acts are eschatological forms of excess – absurdist, avant-gardist, over-the-top gestures foreshadowing a future in which exchange-value will have been surpassed for what Paul Ricoeur terms 'an economy of superabundance.'[60] René Girard sees them as a negative version of potlatch, in which one outshines one's rival not by squandering more goods than he does, but by yielding to him with fine insouciance more than he asks for.[61]

Those who are already camped out on the far edge of history, taking their cue from the future and living in imminent expectation of death, are freed from the need to haggle and negotiate, and can thus be as lavish in their self-expenditure as Gunn's idealised swimmers and fishermen. It is just that their self-dispossession takes the form of giving to others, not of some solitary existential self-expenditure. In *The Principle of Hope*, Ernst Bloch claims that the morality of Jesus is 'the morality of the end of the world', and 'can only be grasped in relation to his kingdom'.[62] In flouting a scrupulously regulated moral economy, it refuses the tit-for-tat logic of the present in a way that is bound to appear folly to those whom Yeats calls hot-faced moneychangers.

Christianity thus combines the moral fervour of the martyr with the laid-back ethics of the hippie. The conjunction is not fortuitous. Those who live as though the future has already arrived pose a threat to the status quo. They are prophets, and as such figures marked out as objects of political violence; yet they also live like the lilies of the field and take no heed for tomorrow. In their touch of surrealist madness and casual way with material necessities, they proclaim the imminence of the reign of justice. If one is heedless of a return for one's gift, it is among other things because an end-time is approaching which will make all such exchange superfluous. Since history is drawing to a close, there is no reason not to give without reserve, like Gunn's swimmers and explorers. Acting and giving must be viewed *sub specie aeternitatis*, deranging the meticulous balance sheets of the present. In this sense, it is less the promise of immortality that spurs one to virtue than the thought of one's mortality. To meditate on one's mortality is to have an opportunity to become truly moral. Revenge, for example, becomes simply not worth pursuing, along with time-consuming schemes for growing fabulously rich at the expense of others. Mercy and forgiveness are ways of inserting the future into the present, anticipating a time in which all odds will be levelled and all debts annulled. Vengeance, by contrast, folds the present and future back into the past, as in Aeschylus's *Oresteia*. While the law of the Furies holds sway, it is impossible to break out of the cycles of retribution and embark upon history proper. Instead, revenge suspends time in a kind of ersatz eternity. It is this fantasy of immortality that lies at the source of so many human woes. 'Man doesn't know how to be mortal', reflects Milan Kundera in his novel *Immortality*.

To take no heed for tomorrow is possible only by living in the knowledge of that ultimate tomorrow which is death. It is an invitation not to forget about time, but to be mindful of the end of time. Jesus, along with some of those who preached his gospel, seemed to have imagined that the kingdom of God was imminent, which proved to be a rather sizeable error. To their mind, history was simply eschatology. The church had simply to stand fast, surrendered in faith to the Lord who was soon to return. Even so, to live *as if* the Day of Judgement were at hand, and thus as if the only pressing matters were justice and fellowship, is not an ethics to be scorned. If there is to be any eternity, it must surely be here and now. 'Eternal life', writes Wittgenstein in the *Tractatus Logico-Philosophicus*, 'belongs to those who live in the present'.[63] And since to live in the present, were it possible, would mean to live out of time, it is a way of anticipating one's death. It is another sense in which, in Eliotic phrase, the moment of death is every moment.

Chapter 4

EXCHANGE AND EXCESS

THE TRUE MARTYR is the one who seeks no return, and there are those who would see this unilateral venturing of the self as the highest ethical act. Jacques Derrida, for example, holds the curious view that the act of giving is ruined by reciprocity. The case reflects his customary libertarian distaste for measure, regulation, identity, equivalence and calculability – unglamorous phenomena, to be sure, but vital to any form of social existence, and not to be dismissed without a certain offensive touch of privilege. The gift for Derrida is what interrupts economy, plays havoc with the coercive and contractual and ruptures the predictable circuit of exchange by putting an end to circulation. Marcel Mauss's *The Gift*, which speaks of the need for gifts to circulate in pre-modern societies, provokes Derrida to an unusually impassioned rebuttal. 'For there to be gift', he writes in *Given Time*, 'there must be no reciprocity, return, exchange, counter-gift, or debt.'[1] One would not have wished to spend Christmas in the Derrida household. 'To refuse the return gift of gratitude from the one to whom one gives', John Milbank comments on this perversely self-indulgent ethics, 'is to celebrate one's will to give ... instead of the miraculous and unpredictable arrival of achieved affinity and surprising reciprocity.'[2] For Rabbi Eleazar ben Pedat, writing in the third century CE, the destruction of the Second Temple in Jerusalem had sundered the intimate link between God and the people of Israel, so that they were now forced to offer their prayers with no expectation of an immediate response. Unlike Derrida, however, he did not greet the situation with acclaim. Unilateralism was the consequence of a grievous alienation.[3]

In Anthony Trollope's novel *Framley Parsonage*, the impoverished but proud-hearted clergyman Crawley tells a friend who offers him charity that 'it is very sweet to give; I do not doubt that. But the taking of what is given is very bitter. Gift bread chokes in a man's throat and poisons his blood, and sits like lead upon the heart.' In Derrida's view, a gift becomes poisonous the moment it places the recipient in debt; yet since gifts cannot avoid such a destiny, they are (in one of his most portentous terms) 'impossible'. Indeed, he considers with solemn absurdity that the fact that a gift is a gift at all must be thrust into oblivion in the act of donation. The most valid offering is thus the one annihilated at the very moment of bestowal, which brings Derrida's case intriguingly close to a traditional concept of sacrifice. A gift which is not acknowledged as such cannot be returned, and is thus the most absolute of offerings. It accomplishes itself in abolishing itself, and in this unconditional status reflects the immortal life of the gods. The Situationists held a similar view, concerned as they were with what one commentator calls 'the subtle art of not returning the donation, of giving again in a way that is not circular, that does not simply pass on the debt'.[4]

Jean-Joseph Goux, however, points out that since one tends to give others what one assumes they will appreciate, the other is already implicated in the gift in a way that qualifies any pure unilateralism.[5] The recipient is implicit in the gift in much the same way that an interlocutor is tacitly present in an act of utterance. Besides, one should not deprive others of occasions to be generous. 'The status of giving', writes Seneca, 'should be that no return ought to be asked, yet that a return is possible.'[6] There is nothing wrong with wistfully expecting a Georgian mansion in return for one's tattered bunch of violets. To do so is not to strike one's own gift valueless. Here as in general, it is not the thought that counts but the action. To give unconditionally is to give whether a return is likely or not, not (as Derrida considers) to give without thinking of one. It is not a question of mental hygiene.

Derrida seems coolly indifferent to the actual nature of a gift, which is another excellent reason, were he still alive, for not spending Christmas with him. 'The gift', he writes, 'is the gift of the giving itself and nothing else.'[7] What one bestows is trumped by the act of giving itself. This is not, however, the case with the lover or the martyr, for whom donor and gift are one, and what might appear the most vacuous act of offering – to yield up nothing but oneself – is in fact the most profound. In sexual love, as in martyrdom, it is one's body one bestows, not (as in ritual sacrifice) some semiotic substitute for it. In this purest form of self-giving, then, the gift itself could not be of greater moment. In any case, what one chooses to donate ought not to be a matter of indifference.[8] One would not offer a bottle of whisky to a recovering alcoholic, or a tarantula to an arachnophobe. Too cavalier a disregard for the specific can be obtuse as well as generous-hearted.

Besides, too extravagant or gratuitous a gesture may sabotage the strict equivalences of justice. 'An eye for an eye and a tooth for a tooth', commonly regarded as a barbaric recipe for vengeance, is intended not as carte blanche for savage reprisal but as a constraint on how much one may exact in recompense for an injury. Since it insists that any such restitution must be proportionate, it is an enlightened injunction in context, as those who dismiss equivalences as coldly calculating might do well to note. Portia's plea for mercy in *The Merchant of Venice* is among other, finer, things a ploy on the part of the Venetian governing elite, of whom this young patrician is self-appointed spokeswoman, to persuade an odious Jewish outsider to waive his legally valid demand for justice from those who have not the slightest intention of granting it. Perhaps Shylock does well to cling so obdurately to his bond, a legal contract into which his debtor Antonio freely entered. Mercy may suspend justice, but it must not be allowed to make a mockery of it. One must beware of forgiving one's enemies or turning the other cheek out of a deep-seated conviction that nothing matters much in any case, a viewpoint close to the hard-boiled cynicism of Lucio in *Measure for Measure*. There can be a worthless kind of mercy, just as there can be a wild kind of justice. Both virtues can be bought on the cheap.

Derrida, then, is too little alert to the possibility of non-contractual exchange. Gifts mutually offered are still gifts. What makes a gift a gift is not spontaneity, non-equivalence or non-reciprocity, but the fact that (at least in modern times) there is no practical reason for handing it over. The gift itself may have a function, but the act of bestowing it does not, other than perhaps as a token of affection. What taints a gift is not reciprocity but the fact that it has a practical motive: to win favour, for example, or advertise one's warm-heartedness. It is utility, not mutuality, that is the ruin of gift-giving, though we shall see in a moment that the giving of gifts in pre-modern cultures may indeed serve some practical end, caught up as it is in a network of social functions and obligations. In modern times, one may feel socially or morally constrained to offer or return a gift, but it is the fact that the custom itself serves no immediate practical purpose that distinguishes it most obviously from most forms of contractual exchange. John Milbank acknowledges this point when he claims that there must be 'an element of freedom' in gift-giving if it is to be distinguished in this way.[9] In his view, giving should be reciprocal, but the offerings in question must be non-identical and the counter-gift should be deferred in time. There should also be an element of surprise.[10] It is not clear, however, why swapping identical pairs of socks at the same moment in an entirely predictable manner should not count as an authentic exchange of gifts; nor is it clear exactly how free one is not to give one's spouse a birthday present. As a non-functional phenomenon, the act of giving resembles a work of art more than it does a sack of potatoes. It is true that in the case of art, the act of production may itself be in a certain sense obligatory, as the artist is required to turn out so many loyal odes, court masques, oratorios or portraits of noble patrons. But the artistic product itself remains non-functional, at least in any immediate practical sense.

Economic production under socialism would be neither free, gratuitous, spontaneous, unnecessary nor, for the most part, non-functional. Yet since it would be undertaken for the sake of the common good rather than for the profit of a minority, one might nonetheless regard it as a form of gift. It would furnish the means of life as an end and value in itself. Production would serve a practical purpose, but it would also have expressive and communicative ends. Moreover, though there would still be exchange under socialism, it would not be governed by the commodity form. In this sense, exchange and the capitalist marketplace are not to be seen as synonymous. A socialist society would not erase the borders between gift-giving, social bonds and material production, but it would blur them.[11]

Kevin Hart makes much the same mistake as Derrida when he comments that 'to be sure, we can aim for vows and community; but if we begin with them we risk not talking about love so much as contract and exchange'.[12] But not all mutuality is contractual, and those modes of it that happen to be so are not always objectionable on that score. 'I can think *agape*', Hart writes, 'only if I rigorously exclude all contract and exchange',[13] a curious view for one who presumably champions the institution of marriage. Shakespeare's *The Merchant of Venice*, for which the word 'bond' signifies both legal contract and fleshly relation, has some acute reflections on this specious distinction between law and love, form and feeling. The oppressed may need a formal bill of rights for their protection, however drearily bureaucratic this may seem to their more privileged fellow citizens. As Shakespeare's play recognises, they would be unwise to rely on the whimsical largesse of their superiors. It is those in command who can afford to dispense with a bill of rights and sing the praises of spontaneity.

Jean-Luc Marion seems to imagine that love involves an encounter between two entirely unilateral acts of self-giving – 'the coincidence of two absolute non-reciprocities', as John Milbank aptly puts it.[14]

Though he does not reject the notion of mutuality out of hand, he appears to suspect it à la Derrida of some disreputable contractualism,[15] a suspicion which even the most cursory phenomenology of love is likely to dispel. It is not only that both partners in a loving relationship give and receive simultaneously, but that the self-giving of each evokes a comparable response in the other, in a process that is both self-augmenting and self-replenishing. 'The more I give to thee, the more I have', as Juliet sighs to Romeo. It is a question of mutuality but not measure, reciprocity but not equivalence. Mutual love has something of the contagiousness of mutual laughter, as the other's delighted response serves only to enhance one's own.

In this dialectic of giving and receiving, it is the latter that is fundamental. It is hardly news that those who were uncherished as children are likely to find the demands of love hard to handle. Thomas Aquinas holds that charity requires one to receive as well as give, while E.M. Forster seems to regard the former as more estimable than the latter. Freud found the seeds of morality in the infant's gratitude to its carers. Nietzsche's Übermensch, by contrast, is munificent in his gifts to others, but too proud to stoop to receiving. His giving is a form of lordship, capricious and condescending, free of anything as despicably petty-bourgeois as obligation or return. From a Christian viewpoint, this is to ignore the fact that to be capable of giving in the first place means to be in receipt of the gift of Being. Before any exchange between human beings can be established, something must already have been donated to make it possible. In this sense, one's dependency on the Other is the ground of both mutual and unilateral offerings.

The oil lavished by Mary Magdalene on the feet of Jesus, to the dismay of the book-balancing Judas, is thus for Christian faith not an affront to thrift but part of a deeper economy, one whose source lies in the reckless self-squandering of God himself. There is a shift from the business of early gift exchange, with its meticulously coded mutualities, to the Christian doctrine of God's unilateral grace, to which no human response can prove equal. 'The notion that man could feed or enrich his Creator', writes F.D. Kidner, 'has no basis in the Law, and is held up to scorn by the Prophets and Psalmists. The giving was, first of all, all on God's side.'[16] It is of the nature of God to be prodigal, ecstatic, overbrimming, one for whom excess is no more than the norm. Alain Badiou speaks of grace as 'governing a multiplicity in excess of itself, one that is indescribable, superabundant relative to itself as well as to the fixed distributions of the law'.[17] Yet though God has no need of a return from his creatures, his grace lies at the source of their own giving and gratitude. In this sense, exchange and gratuitousness, the reciprocal and the unilateral, are not incompatible. They converge, for example, in the Eucharist, in which the mutuality of a shared meal commemorates a gratuitous self-giving.

Marcel Hénaff points out that to see the gift as non-reciprocal is really just the other face of market exchange, and as such remains caught up in its logic.[18] When exchange becomes largely a traffic in commodities, all notions of contract and reciprocity are likely to be tainted by this association, so that the gift, by reaction, is regarded as a matter of random, private generosity. It is a moral rather than an economic affair, an oasis of individual freedom in a soullessly regulated world. Gift-giving is now less a social institution than a state of mind. This is already the case for Seneca, for whom the gift must constitute a disinterested end in itself, in a godlike refusal to calculate returns. Service to others must be its own reward. As Macbeth remarks to Duncan, 'The service and the loyalty I owe, / In doing it, pays itself' (Act I Scene 4). The Wittgenstein of the *Tractatus Logico-Philosophicus* shares this view, though on the basis of a distinction between ethical and empirical realms he was later to abandon. The Stoics' aversion to utility in an increasingly commercialised social order shifts the focus of gift-giving from the tribute itself, and the consequences it might bring in its wake, to the act of giving and the purity of the donor's intention. The benefits of virtuous action in general, Seneca claims in *De Beneficiis*, lie not in its effects but in its sheer performance. Virtue must be its own recompense – not least, as the novelist Henry Fielding might have pointed out, because it is unlikely to receive much other return in our kind of world. In this sense, an autotelism of the gift, for all its apparent generosity of spirit, may have some disquieting moral implications. By the time of John Calvin, the rift between gift and commercial transaction had grown well-nigh unbridgeable. Only God can bestow gifts, leaving the human domain to the rather less glamorous business of work and trade. Grace and faith confront contract and profit across an immeasurable divide. Moreover, since God's grace is entirely unmerited, quite independent of the nature of our conduct, there can be no more mutuality between him and his creatures than there is between a human and a slug.

* * *

Derrida and his disciples assume a commodified view of gift exchange, and then proceed for that reason to dismiss it out of hand.

It is not hard to see how they could have saved themselves this some-what pointless manoeuvre. Reciprocity can only be imagined in contractual terms. But a mutuality of affection or obligation is not the same as an equivalence of commodities. The dialogical is not to be confused with a financial transaction. In some pre-modern cultures, there is no clear distinction between arbitrary gift and obligatory exchange. The interchange of gifts is neither a moral nor an economic affair but a question of social bonding. One might thus call it a practical business, but this is not to suggest that it is a question of commercial self-interest. As a law-governed piece of social symbolism, the offering of presents dismantles the distinction between generosity and obligation. So in a different sense does the law of charity or the duty of hospitality. As Hénaff puts it, 'the purpose of gift exchange is not to be morally sublime through saintly offering but to recognise one another through the back-and-forth circulation of presents'.[19] He speaks accordingly of 'free obligation', as well as of the 'ritually coded, generous reciprocity' of early gift exchange. For Derrida, by contrast, phrases such as 'free obligation' and 'coded generosity' would border on the oxymoronic.

There are echoes of this state of affairs in modern times. In an essay entitled 'Justice and Generosity', Oliver Goldsmith, who hailed from a society yet to enter fully upon modernity, insists that gener-osity, far from being a whimsical, capricious affair, constitutes a moral obligation.[20] His Irish compatriot Edmund Burke speaks in similar vein of 'obligations written in the heart'.[21] In the Hebrew Scriptures, it is mandatory for the Jews to be unstinting in their almsgiving. A surplus over and above the measure is itself normative, rather as for King Lear a certain degree of superfluity is a human necessity. There is no opposition here between niggardly calculation and cavalier profusion. Paul writes in his Letter to the Romans of humanity, having been absolved from its debts, owing nothing but love; but love, though a light enough burden, is nonetheless viewed as obligatory. To return more than has been conferred on you may be a supererogatory duty demanded by the law of love. This, too, is why reciprocity need not imply equivalence.

Marcel Mauss is another who sees giving in pre-modern times as regulated by rigorous laws. In this scrupulously calibrated system of exchanges, there is really no place for a free gift. Sacrifice, for example, is a practice that compels the gods to make a return. To refuse to give to others may be tantamount to declaring war. For Mauss, reciprocity is built into gift giving, not least because gifts have an enigmatic life of their own, and like homing pigeons tend to gravitate to their point of origin. In any case, since they secrete something of the donor's life, retaining them for too long would be perilous, which is one reason why a perpetual circuit of exchange must be set in motion. Presents are in some sense alive, which is why they should be handled with care, treated with tact and relinquished as soon as possible. It is dangerous for the great networks of mutual donation to grow stagnant. Giving is a form of semiosis, converting a piece of the world into a sign. To offer a gift is to gather a fragment of material reality into the intricate mesh of human meaning, converting matter into a mode of communication. Everything – women, children, food, property, land, rank, labour – is in ceaseless circulation, a sign traced through with the identity of the giver, ephemeral in its very essence, flourishing only in its transmissibility. Gifts are less objects than enunciations. To hoard is thus a cardinal crime, as St James's savage polemic against the well heeled makes clear: 'Come now, you rich, weep and howl for the miseries that are coming upon you! Your riches are corrupted and your garments are moth-eaten. Your gold and silver are corroded, and their corrosion will be a witness against you and will eat your flesh like fire' (James 5:1–3).

Objects in this sense may be permanently on loan, or considered to be yours only on condition that you hand them on.[22] As Segismundo comments in Pedro Calderón de la Barca's *Life is a Dream*, 'what we have is ours only on account', and part of the point of a gift is to alter our view of those possessions to which we imagine we have a right. The gift must be seen as a legacy to the future. Existence is enriched by being expended. We have no reason to be puffed up with the things that surround us, Seneca observes in his *On Consolation to Marcia*, since they have been merely lent to us.[23] The ancient Romans held that one genuinely possessed only what one could give away. Alienability was a mark of proprietorship. 'Life', writes Carlin Barton,

> was a treasure that gained value or power only when expended
> . . . the chosen, the voluntary, the generous death was the extreme
> renunciation that put a high charge on life. It was the renuncia-
> tion that enhanced life, that enhanced the value of a thing being
> renounced. Moreover, the chosen death sacralised, empowered
> the person or thing or value on which it was spent . . . self-
> destruction was the supreme form of munificence, the extremes
> of largesse and deprivation at once.[24]

From this perspective, freely to abnegate one's existence is to live most abundantly. Your life is most intensely yours when it is yours to yield up.

Ritual sacrifice is among other things a critique of proprietorship. In returning a thing to the gods, one proclaims the provisional nature of all ownership. Only by contemplating the potential disappearance of a thing can one grasp its transient nature, and thus know it for what it is. Only by bursting the grape can Keats savour its delectable fullness. Besides, as we have seen, the personal existence that enables you to offer gifts in the first place is itself a gift, on loan from the Other. The donor himself is given to himself by others. 'Men approaching the gods', writes Maurice Godelier, 'are already in their debt, since it is from them that they have already received the conditions for their existence.'[25] The gods are the transcendental condition of all giving, and as such both the cause and object of it. In this version of sacrifice, then, the donor returns a piece of being back to its source in order to demonstrate that it was his only by proxy in the first place, as well as to manifest his faith that it will be restored to him in different guise. This is not the kind of reciprocity to be found in the marketplace. Even so, market exchanges themselves always presuppose a network of symbolic commitments – of trust, loyalty, good faith and so on – which transcend their own utilitarian logic but which also constitute an essential precondition of it.

* * *

John Milbank is surely right to claim that unilateral giving without thought of return, so often proposed as the very apogee of the good, is not so fine a thing as reciprocity.[26] This is not to suggest that such unilateralism has no place. A strain of carnivalesque recklessness, one which scrambles equivalences, upends hierarchies and plays havoc with precise gradations, is central to the Christian Gospel. Its spirit is captured by the sagacious folly of William Blake's *Proverbs of Hell*, with their insistence that the road of excess leads to the palace of wisdom. It is a replication in the ethical realm of the groundless nature of Creation itself, what the philosopher Quentin Meillassoux calls the 'manifest gratuitousness of the given'.[27] Giving without calculation, which finally lies beyond the sphere of the ethical, is at the root of a world within which giving as ethical is possible. Ian Bradley speaks of Yahweh 'as the one who gives himself in a careless and costly way to his people'.[28] Pseudo-Denys describes the goodness of God as ecstatic, excessive and hyperbolic. Meister Eckhart sees it as a seething or boiling over, while Aquinas speaks of the divine nature as *maxime liberalis*. In our own time, the philosopher Stephen Mulhall captures something of the scandalous extremism of Christianity when he writes of the kind of love that

> demands the renunciation of those reciprocal claims that human beings normally and legitimately advance in the context of a loving relationship with others, as the believer places no limits on her responses to her neighbour's claims on her, does not expect reciprocation or consideration from her, does not resent ingratitude, deceit or betrayal. Her love is independent of the way things go, unchanging and immune from defeat . . .[29]

It is this strange, impossible, implacably unconditional love – a process without a subject, one might suggest in Althusserian idiom – which helps to distinguish Christian ethics from the liberal-humanist kind.

The Situationists, who were intrigued by the notion of a gift without return, occasionally gave away their periodical free of charge. Their forerunners, the Lettrist International, revealingly entitled their own journal *Potlatch*.[30] Potlatch is another illustration of how reciprocity need not imply equivalence, involving as it does what one might call a spiral of excessive exchange. As such, it dismantles the distinction between tit-for-tat and overriding the measure. The gifts munificently bestowed by the other must at all costs be returned, but the point is for each donor to outdo the other, in what Jacques Derrida aptly terms 'a sacrificial bidding war'.[31] In the surreal logic of potlatch, the more you give, the more you gain. Much the same is true of sacrifice. He who wins is he who ends up with the emptiest hands. 'To sacrifice', writes Godelier, 'is to give by destroying what is given.'[32] In the act of yielding a thing up to death, nothing is held in reserve. Instead, it is a question of total, irreversible self-expenditure. In this sense, the act of destruction has an extravagance about it which is strangely akin to an abundance of life.

Carlin Barton speaks of the 'potlatch mentality' of ancient Rome, for which profligate giving was a sign of one's abundant wealth and copious vitality.[33] To deplete the self is a token of its formidable power. Jean-Joseph Goux writes of the ancient notion of *munus*, meaning 'an excessive liberality, pompous generosity, public and ostentatious splendor',[34] and sees this extravagance as a form of hauteur. It reflects the desire of the donor to humiliate the receiver. The madcap generosity of potlatch is a ferociously agonistic affair. As such, it represents a satirical send-up of genuine self-dispossession. In a dizzying spiral of credit and debt, one must repay what has been bestowed at an ever-accumulating rate of interest, in fruitless pursuit of the impossible gift for which there could be no conceivable recompense. Wealth is exchanged for power, the economic traded for the political, as canoes are gratuitously smashed, villages burnt to the ground, dog teams slaughtered and copper ingots tossed casually into the ocean. In the custom of potlatch, comments Georges Bataille, the giver 'enriches himself with a contempt for riches'.[35]

Neither Bataille nor Derrida seems sufficiently alert to the fact that there are morally discreditable forms of superfluity. The violent self-squandering of Dionysian ecstasy, reckless and death-haunted, is a case in point. One would not wish to appear in the dock before a judge for whom the principle of equivalence was a despicable instance of petty-bourgeois ideology. Even W.B. Yeats, a poet who in Nietzschean style contrasts the open-handed *sprezzatura* of the aristocrat with the niggardly calculus of the merchant and clerk, takes leave to wonder whether an excess of love might have driven the rebels of Easter 1916 to their deaths. The work of Shakespeare meditates continually on the hair-thin line between creative kinds of superfluity and ruinous forms of excess. It is in *King Lear*, with its ringing of changes on the notions of all, something, nothing, everything, too little and too much, that this investigation is most searching.

Timon of Athens, however, is Shakespeare's most compelling account of how the warm-hearted spendthrift can be a monstrous egoist in disguise. There is a destructive quality to the protagonist's legendary open-handedness:

Plutus, the god of gold,
Is but his steward; no meed but he repays

Sevenfold above itself; no gift to him
But breeds the giver a return exceeding
All use of quittance. (Act I Scene 1)

This is potlatch with a vengeance. Timon's sumptuous expenditure is calculated to daunt and diminish, reducing all rival donors to beggars. His ostentatious giving is among other things a canny way of forestalling the generous impulses of others. Unlike E.M. Forster's highest ethical type, he is ignorant of how to receive, a condition that would involve the indignity of becoming the object of another's agency. Timon's conception of a gift is full-bloodedly Derridean: 'there's none / Can truly say he gives, if he receives', he remarks. The irony is that promiscuous giving, of the kind that steamrollers all specificity, is as indifferent to particular persons, objects, qualities and deserts as the commodity form itself. Like the commodity, it is a species of abstraction. It is also a devious form of self-flattery. 'Bad' forms of generosity distend the self and devalue the world in the same act. To be ready to bestow anything upon anybody is to cheapen your bounty in the act of flaunting it. Giving to all is a matter of caring for none. Moreover, such exorbitant gestures can come to bind others hand and foot, burdening them with a debt which they must struggle to discharge. Benefits that cannot be repaid, observes Samuel Johnson in an essay on friendship, are not commonly found to increase affection. Like sentimentalism, reckless liberality is secretly a form of self-indulgence, and in Timon's case turns out to be literally self-consuming. His spendthrift habits lead to his bankruptcy, plunging him into a peevish misanthropy which is every bit as indifferent to specific qualities as his erstwhile beneficence. It is self-expenditure of this kind that Friedrich Nietzsche found particularly distasteful. Rich and generous souls who spend themselves lavishly, almost indifferently, he writes in *Beyond Good and Evil*, can thereby inflate the virtue of generosity into a vice. Instead, one must learn how to conserve oneself, reining in one's superabundant powers with the severity and self-discipline of the Übermensch. To give well, teaches Zarathustra, is an art; but he pronounces these words in rebuke of one who, ashamed of his riches, lavishes them on the ungrateful poor.[36]

*   *   *

The most strikingly gratuitous act is that of forgiveness, which ruptures the reciprocities of justice or the eternal cycles of vengeance, introducing a certain constructive non-identity into their fearful symmetry. The power of mimesis is accordingly broken: what I do is not what you do. Hegel describes the act as 'the cancellation of fate'. *Dialectic of Enlightenment* views ancient sacrifice as foreshadowing the modern principle of exchange, which in the moral sphere takes the form of a fruitless circuit of sin, guilt and expiation. It is also the tit-for-tat reciprocity of justice, which exacts a condign penalty for each offence, as well as the 'wild justice' of revenge. For Christian faith, it is God's refusal of this sterile principle that overthrows the *ancien régime* and inaugurates a new order, one in which equivalence gives way to excess. Forgiveness is the enemy of exchange value.

What breaks this circuit on Calvary is the fact that crime and forgiveness are one. In homeopathic mode, poison and cure are aspects of the same reality, as they are in the case of the scapegoat. The execution of Jesus involves the unjust spilling of human blood;

but since it is also the act of pardoning it, the stalled dialectic of action and reaction – of crime, guilt, sacrifice, reparation and yet more crime – is brought to a close. The sin of the world is concentrated in the Cross in order to be forgiven there. What is now normative – grace – is what overflows the measure, an *acte gratuit* beyond all equity and even-handedness, a bounteousness that defeats all calibration.

The idea of forgiveness is not easy to grasp. It does not mean to forget, or even to behave as though one has forgotten. The injunction to forgive and forget is not only implausible but absurd. You might manage to forgive whoever murdered your child, but you are hardly likely to wipe the event from memory. On the contrary, forgiveness is more a matter of remembrance, in the Freudian sense of the word, than oblivion. It requires you to actively confront and relive the past, not least to avoid being enslaved by it in the manner of the neurotic. Otherwise one remains perpetually in thrall to the offender, unable to prise oneself free from his deed, and to that extent the puppet of one's personal history. If those who offend can be forgiven, it is partly because they, too, are the products of a situation not of their own making. 'Father, forgive them for they know not what they do' is an appeal for mercy and forgiveness based on a recognition of false consciousness. One may note, however, that there is a difference between the two acts. One may be merciful without having been offended (as a judge, for example), but one cannot forgive without having been offended.

To forgive is not necessarily to exculpate. It does not involve refusing moral judgement in some bogus bout of generous-mindedness. Nor does it necessarily mean setting aside the claims of justice. You can let an offender off scot-free, but it is not incompatible with forgiveness to insist that the guilty party makes reparation for his misdeeds. Thomas Aquinas sees no discrepancy between forgiveness and the demand for restitution. As John Milbank argues, forgiveness – the 'gift to the undeserving' – is not for high medieval theology a grandly unilateral gesture, a forgoing or form of negativity, but a 'justice beyond justice', a positive matter of restitution and reconciliation based on a mutual agreement as to the rectification of past faults and the appropriate distribution of deserts. It is partly through restitution, and therefore through justice, that the reconciliation of the wrongdoer and the wronged can be accomplished, and forgiveness thus sealed.[37]

In this sense, forgiveness differs from the whimsical fiat of an absolute monarch who sweeps aside due legal process. Pardoning others need not depend on their being suitably penitent. No doubt Jesus would have welcomed some show of contrition from the unsavoury types with whom he consorts, but he seems not to have insisted on it as a condition of enjoying their company. Nor does he require them to demonstrate their remorse by making sacrifice, as the religious conventions of the time demanded.[38] Instead, in strikingly heterodox fashion, he eats with morally disreputable men and women without first demanding that they change their ways. His forgiveness would seem to be unconditional. Perhaps he considered that sinners had no time to mend their ways, given the imminent arrival of the kingdom. His absolute stance on forgiveness is a foreshadowing of that event.

Jesus not only demands forgiveness for those who persist in their wrongdoing, which is to say those who place themselves like the

Gentiles permanently outside the Law, but scandalously suggests that these reprobates will take priority over the righteous in entering the kingdom of God. It is the crooks and whores of the highways who will assume pride of place at the celestial wedding feast. Heaven is by no means a meritocracy. Instead, it makes a mockery of the scrupulous computations of this world. Divine accountancy, like that of some transnational corporations, is of a different order from the common-or-garden variety. 'God is no respecter of persons', remarks a character in August Strindberg's drama *Miss Julie*, meaning no respecter of social rank.

To pardon a wrong does not necessarily mean to feel warmly towards the offender. To treat those who have harmed you charitably involves helping them to thrive, attending to their welfare, doing them good rather than injury, refraining from treating them vindictively and trying not to feel bitter about the injuries they have inflicted. It might also involve reflecting on how, in similar circumstances, one might have behaved in much the same way. In this sense, forgiveness involves a degree of realism about human frailty, as Shakespeare's *Measure for Measure* (a play whose title announces its concern with exchange value) is aware. Use every man after his desert, as Hamlet remarks to Polonius, and who shall escape whipping? Jacques Lacan speaks of loving the other in so far as she is lacking. To show mercy is to have insight into the moral weakness of the offender, thus acknowledging one's solidarity with him. *Measure for Measure* posits an affinity between love and knowledge in just this sense. Whereas love as *eros* is typically ensnared in fantasy, love as *caritas* requires a well-nigh impossible lucidity of vision – one, to be sure, which is never entirely dissociable from the heart-warming illusions of the erotic.

127

To forgive your enemies does not mean that you are obliged to hold them in high esteem, still less to invite them round to dinner every evening. Like turning the other cheek, it is a condition of fruitful inaction, not in the first place a state of mind. By returning nothing for something, something can come of nothing, despite Lear's minatory words to his youngest daughter. In this sense, forgiveness imitates the act of Creation, which Jean-Luc Nancy calls 'a fortuitous rupture in nothingness'[39] – though as a form of creative undoing there is also a sense in which it consigns something to nothing, as Kierkegaard comments in his *Works of Love*, and can thus be seen also as a reversal of the Creation as well as a repetition of it. It involves not retaliating, thus breaking the sealed circuit of ethical exchange value and bringing to birth a radically new situation. As such, it is a supreme example of Alain Badiou's celebrated event, which appears to spring from nowhere and which in doing so transforms the context from which it emerges.[40] Events of this kind are quasi-miraculous occurrences, without much mundane rhyme or reason, and there are occasions when forgiveness would seem to call for just such a miracle too. What the New Testament commands is surely an affront to flesh and blood. How could one possibly forgive the rapist of one's young daughter? This is why the act is traditionally thought to require the grace of God. Radical forgiveness is probably beyond our power. It is not of this world. The unconditional is the prerogative of the divine. One reason why forgiveness is so difficult is that small children have yet to become capable of it, and small children are to a large extent what we remain.

Even so, forgiveness permits us a glimpse of what would be needed to alter our condition. If it is ultimately beyond our power in the present, it is nevertheless a token of the future. Actively to relinquish your title to strike back involves a kind of *Gelassenheit*, or conscious letting be, and as such is a species of sacrifice or renunciation. Indeed, it involves renouncing one of the most pleasurable of experiences: revenge. As the etymology of the word would suggest, forgiveness is a form of forgoing – a species of wise passiveness which refuses to insist on what is due to it in the knowledge that such action is likely to breed reaction, and so on in a fateful cycle. As an African chief remarks in Saul Bellow's novel *Henderson the Rain King*,

> [A brave man] will not want to live by passing on the wrath [of an offence committed against him]. A hit B? B hit C? – we have not enough alphabet to cover the condition ... He shall keep the blow. No man shall get it from him, and that is a sublime ambition.

To absorb a trespass rather than pass it on is one function of the scapegoat. Besides, if everyone is at once victim and offender, why not allow this sterile dialectic to cancel all the way through into a reciprocity of pardon, as mutual reproach yields to a common acceptance of infirmity?

*   *   *

Let us turn now to five literary cameos of forgiveness. When Anna Karenina leaves her bloodless bureaucrat of a husband for a doomed relationship with the dashing Vronsky, Karenin's first thoughts are of vengeance. Yet when he is called to Anna's sickbed in the belief that she is dying, this vindictive impulse melts into pity and compassion:

a glad feeling of love and forgiveness for his enemies filled his heart. He knelt down and laying his head in the curve of her arm, which burned like fire through her sleeve, he sobbed like a child . . . his pity for her, and remorse at having desired her death, and, most of all, the joy of forgiving suddenly gave him not only relief from his own sufferings but an inward peace such as he had never known before. He suddenly felt that the very thing that was the source of his sufferings had become the source of his spiritual joy; that what had appeared insoluble so long as he indulged in censure, recriminations and hatred, had become simple and clear when he forgave and loved.

The act of forgiveness is both liberating and luminously clarifying. By portraying this priggish state functionary in a morally admirable light, the novel artfully overturns the reader's expectations, inviting us to sympathise just when we were prepared to censure. Karenin, too, has an inner life, however emotionally arthritic he may be. Perhaps the glamorous Vronsky, had he been in the shoes of the man he cuckolds, would have proved no match for his moral fibre. Rather as *Middlemarch* shows the emotionally anaemic Casaubon to be worthy of our sympathy, unsettling the reader's too-easy stereotyping, so Tolstoy morally re-educates his audience by allowing them to see that the most glacially aloof of characters can be as wounded by sexual betrayal as the most emotionally vulnerable.

Sammy Mountjoy, the protagonist of William Golding's *Free Fall*, is in search of the elusive moment in time when he lost his freedom. To do so, he must unpick the complex narrative of cause and effect that constitutes his career to date. Sammy is caught up with others in a network of love and guilt, debt and desire, action and reaction, a social unconscious in which actions breed injurious effects far beyond what they may intend. 'People don't seem to be able to move without killing each other', one of his friends complains. 'We are neither the innocent nor the wicked', Sammy remarks, 'we are the guilty. We fall down. We crawl on hands and knees. We weep and tear each other.' This web of inescapable mutual injury, into which we are born as guilty innocents without ever being given a choice in the matter, is what Christianity knows as original sin; and Sammy is resolved to 'break the awful line of descent' by fumbling back along its densely braided strands for the point where he became ensnared in them beyond all apparent hope of redemption. Yet there is no such definitive moment. The Fall has always already happened. The web can always be unravelled back further in time, or tracked further out in space. Hence Jacques Derrida's infamous, incontestable claim that there is nothing beyond the reach of textuality, a remark which has nothing to do with writing. *Free Fall* itself curves back and forth in time, circling to pinpoint the moment of its hero's loss of freedom rather than offering us a linear narrative.

Intent on repairing some of the damage, Sammy visits Miss Pringle, a sadistic schoolmistress who treated him cruelly as a child, in order to grant her forgiveness. But the schoolmistress has disavowed her own brutality and escaped into innocence, thereby leaving her former pupil with his guilt still on his head. Without her act of repentance, his pardon is worthless. The innocent cannot forgive, the novel reflects, because they do not know that they have been offended; but neither can the more disingenuous members of the ranks of the guilty, who like Miss Pringle have denied ownership of their misdemeanours and so, in leaving their victims unassuaged, torture them for a second time. The dead cannot forgive either, which is why so many political crimes must go unshriven. When it comes to forgiveness, there is a sense in which to offend others is to place oneself at their mercy, so that it is those we injure who now have the upper hand.

It is not here, however, that Sammy stumbles upon his freedom. It is when he is locked in a room in a Nazi prison camp, half-crazed with fear at the presence of some slimy, obscene horror at its centre – a heart collapsed in its own blood, perhaps, or a severed phallus – and is then, for no apparent reason, suddenly released: 'Rising from my knees, holding my trousers huddled I walked uncertainly out towards the judge. But the judge had gone.' The Nazi officer who had been interrogating Mountjoy, along with the whole imposing paraphernalia of law, crime and punishment that he represents, has been whisked away like so much stage scenery, to leave a world without judges which is at once flatly familiar and transfigured beyond all recognition. Sammy's inquisitor has been replaced by an officer who apologises for his colleague's harsh treatment of him. The slimy horror on the floor of the cell turns out to be a damp floor cloth.

Robert Merivel, the hero of Rose Tremain's novel *Restoration*, is a gentleman at the court of Charles II who loses the king's favour and is accordingly deprived of his country mansion. From a foppish existence at court, where he is granted the role of the king's unofficial Fool, he moves to a Quaker hospital, where he lives a life of austere self-denial and puts his medical skills to use among the poor. He later saves a woman's life in the Great Fire of London. As a result, Charles summons him unexpectedly to his former country house and tells him that he may take possession of it once again, 'in return for the life you have saved and the man you have become'. Formally speaking, the act is one of restoration, as Merivel receives back part of what he has lost in an equitable exchange of virtue for property. Its true significance, however, lies in the restoration of the king's affection for his wayward subject, a love that in Merivel's eyes is beyond price. He has been matured by his misfortunes to the point where he no longer entertains any callow expectations of regaining Charles's good will; and it is precisely at this point that the king's favour is bestowed on him. If the innocent cannot forgive, the foolish cannot appreciate the worth of what they have. Through loss and affliction, Merivel comes in the end to do just that.

Patrick Melrose, the protagonist of Edward St Aubyn's *At Last*, was sexually assaulted by his father as a child, and is teetering on the verge of psychological collapse. In the final pages of the novel, however, he breaks through to a new self-understanding:

Perhaps whatever he thought he couldn't stand was made up partly or entirely of the thought that he couldn't stand it. He didn't really know, but he had to find out, and so he opened himself up to the feeling of utter helplessness and incoherence that he supposed he had spent his life trying to avoid, and waited for it to dismember him. What happened was not what he expected. Instead of feeling the helplessness, he felt the helplessness and compassion for the helplessness at the same time. One followed the other swiftly, just as if he had reached out instinctively to rub a hit shin, or relieve an aching shoulder. He was after all not an infant, but a man experiencing the chaos of infancy welling up in his conscious mind. As the compassion expanded he saw himself on equal terms with his supposed persecutors, saw his parents, who appeared to be the cause of his suffering, as unhappy children with parents who appeared to be the cause of their suffering: there was no one to blame and everyone to help, and those who appeared to deserve the most blame needed the most help. For a while he stayed level with the pure inevitability of things being as they were, the ground zero of events on which the sky-scrapers of personal experience were built, and as he imagined not taking his life so personally, the heavy impenetrable darkness of the inarticulacy turned into a silence that was perfectly transparent, and he saw that there was a margin of freedom, a suspension of reaction, in that clarity.

Patrick slid back in his chair and sprawled in front of the view. He noticed how his tears cooled as they ran down his cheeks. Washed eyes and a tired and empty feeling. Was that what people meant by peaceful? There must be more to it than that, but he didn't claim to be an expert. He suddenly wanted to see his children, real children, not the ghosts of their ancestors' childhoods, real children with a reasonable chance of enjoying their lives. He picked up the phone and dialled Mary's number.

Patrick can finally forgive his parents by an acknowledgement of original sin. They, too, were caught up in an anonymous web of damage, debt, guilt and blame, one without source or goal. Like Lacanian desire, this condition is nothing personal, and Melrose must try to take his own life less personally if he is to be set free. Like him, his parents were legatees of the failings of their own forebears, who continued to inhabit their psyches like unquiet ghosts, and who linger on in Patrick himself and his dealings with others. 'In a broad sense', writes Adrian Poole, 'tragedy always deals with toxic matter bequeathed by the past to the present.'[41] Owing to the state of original sin, it is impossible to reckon up how many individuals there are in any given relationship. Patrick's ghastly parents were enmeshed like him in an awful line of descent for which they were only partly responsible; and the distancing gaze by which he is able to recognise this, 'not taking his life so personally', also releases in him a certain therapeutic pity for himself. To see his own fate as bound up with the destiny of others is to stand for a moment outside his own cheerless existence, and both the distance and the sense of common involvement are essential for self-forgiveness. By virtue of the same self-distancing, he can now distinguish the adult in himself from the infant, separating the two while acknowledging a continuity of wretchedness between them. It is not that as an adult he can now master the infant's sense of chaos, but that he is able for a moment to surrender himself to that terror precisely as an adult, a free decision of which the infant would be incapable. By consciously reliving his tormented childhood, he can begin to move beyond it. Through a 'suspension of reaction', he can finally free himself from the ancestral chains that bind him.

Kate Croy and Merton Densher of Henry James's *The Wings of the Dove* are a young couple in love but without the means to marry. They befriend a fabulously rich young American woman, Milly Theale, whom Kate discovers to be terminally ill. Kate persuades Densher to pay court to Milly, who has fallen in love with him, so that Milly and Densher may marry and the Englishman inherit the

American's wealth when she dies. Milly is told of the plot against her on her deathbed, but nevertheless bequeaths her fortune to Densher. The effect of this astonishing *acte gratuit* is to cause Densher to fall passionately in love with Milly's memory. Remorseful for his and Kate's plotting, he refuses to accept the heiress's bequest. Kate, suspecting that Densher is in love with the dead woman, insists that she will marry him only if he accepts Milly's fortune, thus testifying that he has put his devotion to her behind him. For his part, Densher is willing to marry Kate, but only without Milly's fortune. If Kate should choose not to marry him, he will make the legacy over to her. Unable to resolve this deadlock, he and Kate part for ever.

Milly's beautifully disinterested action is a perfect instance of gratuitous, unilateral giving, as well as of forgiveness. In James's fiction, doing nothing (in this case, Milly's refusal to repay Kate and Densher in their own moral coin) often enough constitutes the most momentous event in a narrative – the lack, absence, refusal or absten-tion on which an entire drama turns. Indeed, writing itself was for James a form of creative abstention from action. Milly's extraordi-nary act is both nothing at all – a saintly refusal to retaliate – and surreally excessive, thus defeating measure in two opposite direc-tions. The same is true of the wealth she bestows, which is mere inert stuff in itself but a breeder of well-nigh infinite possibilities. In James's writing, money can yield you an abundance of life, but it also makes you the target of predatory adventurers. It is at once blessed and cursed.

That Milly's act is an event in a Badiou-like sense seems recog-nised *avant la lettre* by James himself, who capitalises the word in the novel's appendix. Since death levels all debts and makes all odds even, it is a suitable moment at which to undercut exchange value and inaugurate a startlingly unforeseeable happening, one which breaks abruptly through conventional expectations and turns Kate and Densher's world upside down. Milly is Kate and Densher's sacrificial dove, but by meekly embracing this role she ends up triumphantly transcending it. A dove may be vulnerable, but it is also soaring and buoyant, able to give the slip to its earthbound captors. Milly's prodigal act of giving may be contrasted with Kate's scrupulously calculated sacrifice in handing Densher over to her rival, a self-denial entered into entirely with an eye to its advantages. The words 'Milly' and 'money' constitute a para-rhyme, and the two in Kate's eyes are more or less identical. This is not the case with Densher, however, who desires Milly rather than the money, and therefore loses Kate along with his fortune. As Georges Bataille writes, one who makes sacrifice destroys the offering in order 'to give up the wealth that the victim could have been for him.'[42]

Milly's act is pure partly because it can have no consequences for herself, and thus seems absolved of self-interest. She does not even profit from Densher's gratitude, since she will be dead by the time he learns of her munificence. She dies as a kind of martyr, bequeathing her death to Densher, using it to bring fulfilment to the man she loves. And since this will take the form of Densher's being able to marry Kate, Milly's dying act represents a double pardon. As one who has lived for years with death in her bones, she is unlikely to be disarmed by the event when it finally arrives. She is thus able to make something rich and rare of her dying. Having known in her illness a kind of death-in-life, she can convert this condition on her deathbed into a form of life-in-death. Art itself is in James's view a species of life-in-death or perpetual self-immolation, which means that the act of writing the novel is at one with its preoccupations. Renunciation is one of his abiding motifs. What Milly has to give – her wealth – is trifling compared to the love with which she yields it up, so that the act of bequeathing beggars the bequest itself. Her gift must substitute itself for the devotion that inspired it. Her money is all she can now hand on. In this sense, it is the widow's mite.

Yet Milly's gift is in a sense returned. It is restored in Densher's loving, guilt-stricken refusal to accept it. 'Something had happened to him', James writes, 'too beautiful and sacred to describe. He had been, to his recovered sense, forgiven, dedicated, blessed . . .' In a negative reciprocity, a non-response evokes a non-acceptance. Yet purely unilateral acts are hard to come by. Like any other event, they enter into the tangled web of cause and consequence to breed incalculable effects there, rather as Kate's own scrupulously gauged actions finally spin beyond her control. You cannot predetermine what meaning your action will have for the Other. Whether she intends it or not, Milly's self-forfeiture has the most fateful results for her companions, if not for herself. In its sublime transcendence of self-interest, this morally admirable, aesthetically resplendent gesture succeeds in breaking up Kate and Densher as surely as might a prolonged bout of sexual infidelity.

The question, then, is whether Milly had foreseen this possibility. Is she a saint or a schemer?[43] There are, after all, a number of other apparently admirable young women in James's fiction (Fleda Vetch in *The Spoils of Poynton*, the paranoid governess of *The Turn of the Screw*, Maggie Verver of *The Golden Bowl*) who may be far from the morally blameless figures they present to a credulous world. 'Gift-giving', writes Maurice Godelier, 'can be, simultaneously or successively, an act of generosity or of violence.'[44] Is Milly's liberality a devious act of aggression? Is the finest vengeance to forgo revenge? Does she behave as bountifully as she does in order to put Kate in the moral shade, snatch Densher from her clutches, secure his undying affection and in doing so punish this treasonable lover with a lifetime of loss and remorse? Is his penalty for deceiving her to be besotted for the rest of his life with a corpse? Even if the dying woman did not premeditate all of this – a foresight that would require a degree of moral intricacy remarkable even for a Jamesian protagonist – her gift might still be seen as a gesture of moral superiority. In any case, if it is spontaneous rather than calculated, how morally admirable is an indifference to the potentially injurious effects of one's conduct on others?

As often with James, the issue is undecidable. The novel carefully allows us no access to its heroine's motives. It is hard to say whether self-sacrifice is altruism or egoism, a humbling of the self or a final truculent assertion of it. Perhaps, as a critic once remarked of Samuel Richardson's Pamela, James's heroine is scheming, but unconsciously so. Or perhaps, disciplined by the death she bears within her body, she simply moves in a different moral world from her two less reputable companions. Maybe her act is pure, but with a 'pathological' taint. She herself may have no more idea than the reader how truly dispassionate it is. In any case, if Milly had really set Densher up for life, how much would her motives matter, since his remorse suggests that he is worthy of such a favour? Yet it is possible that, had Milly been able to witness the destructive results of her action, she might have judged it to have gone disastrously awry. One of the drawbacks of actions performed at the point of death is that you are no longer around to repair the damage should they backfire. But it is not certain that Milly would have been dismayed by what transpires.

Even the least conditional of gifts, so the novel suggests, can place one under a crippling moral obligation. Such debts are what sets in motion the endless cycles of sacrifice. Giving can be a hazardous business. It can forge an irrevocable bond between donor and recipient which neither party may desire, and which may ultimately bring both of them to grief. Some modern corporations have taken to awarding their employees pay rises in the form of a gift, in order to win their gratitude and motivate them to work harder.[45] One business commentator has even suggested that products should be given away free, so as to inspire greater loyalty among customers and induce them to buy more.[46] In some tribal societies, so Marcel Mauss informs us, a wariness of gifts is demonstrated by throwing them to the ground in an act of ritual mistrust. To give may well be to gain a hold over the beneficiary. A debt that cannot be discharged because the creditor is dead, or ignorant of the obligation, can fasten an infinite burden on the self. Perhaps there are no donations without strings attached, even if the donor does not fasten them herself. Perhaps all gifts are to some degree poisoned, as the etymology of the word would suggest. Forgiveness is likewise a perilous affair. It can simply deepen the guilt of those who are granted it, holding them permanently in thrall to an unpayable debt, as it seems likely to do with Densher at the end of James's novel. He is now leashed ineluctably to Milly's death, frozen at the still point of her pardon.

If Milly is a sacrificial dove, she is also a kind of scapegoat. It is as though she takes Kate and Densher's transgressions on her own head and bears them off with her into death. Like the scapegoat, she is a redemptive creature, a tutelary deity whose wings hover protectively over her faithless friends, turning their greed and duplicity into an opportunity for new life. It is to the subject of scapegoating that we can now turn.

Chapter 5

KINGS AND BEGGARS

THE PROPHET ISAIAH speaks movingly of a figure known as
the Servant of Yahweh, seen by some scholars as a prototype of
Christ:

> Surely he has borne our infirmities
> and carried our diseases;
> yet we accounted him stricken,
> struck down by God, and afflicted.
> But he was wounded for our transgressions,
> crushed for our iniquities;
> upon him was the punishment that made us whole,
> and by his bruises we are healed. (Isaiah 53:4–5)

The figure in question is the scapegoat, the one on whom the community loads its crimes so that it may be ritually purged.[1] This involves a
curious form of exchange: the more polluted the scapegoat, the purer
the polis. The dooming of the scapegoat is the redemption of the
community. The modern age, by contrast, takes a more individualised

view of moral sickness. 'We are all ill, with one malaise or another', writes José Saramago in *The Year of the Death of Ricardo Reis*, 'a deep-rooted malaise that is inseparable from what we are and that somehow makes us what we are, you might even say that each one of us is his own illness . . .' Or as Samuel Beckett puts it in *The Unnamable*, 'Ah a nice mess we're in the whole pack of us, is it possible we're all in the same boat, no, we're in a nice mess each in his own peculiar way.'

The scapegoat or *pharmakos* also involves another curious ambiguity, which is that the more besmirched it becomes, staggering under the burden of transgressions heaped on its head, the more admirably selfless it shows itself to be. Its redemptive power grows as its identification with human sin deepens, which is one reason why this sacrificial beast, like all sacred things, is both blessed and cursed. The scapegoat is an unthinkable animal, at once guilty and innocent, poison and cure. This homeopathic creature cleanses by being contaminated. It is not sinful in itself, but as St Paul says of Christ, it is 'made sin' for the sake of others. 'Christ redeemed us from the curse of the Law', Paul writes in Galatians, 'having become a curse for us' (Galatians 3:13). 'The one who has suffered so much', Jean-Joseph Goux writes of Oedipus, 'who has become the most degraded, the most rejected of men, will also be a source of perpetual benediction for the people who welcome his tomb.'[2] Rather as the martyr plucks something of value from a blighted condition, so the scapegoat is a device for transmuting guilt into innocence, or sin into saintliness. Because it is constituted by the traces of others as a motley collection of their misdemeanours, it lacks all being in itself; but this mode of non-being can exert a peculiar potency among the living.

The patchwork nature of the creature, unlike most postmodern forms of hybridity, hints at a kind of commonality. It represents the point at which men and women converge in their shared unregeneracy. At least we have our crimes in common, as a solid ground on which to build some less discreditable form of mutual belonging. The negative solidarity signified by the *pharmakos*, the state of original sin in which men and women are bound involuntarily together in mutual guilt and injury, must furnish the foundation for some more positive form of reciprocity. Only then can the scapegoat as monster become the scapegoat as saviour. As a de-differentiating power, this hideous creature is a sign of our shared humanity, which is finally more fundamental than the distinctions which mark it. Derek Parfit's magisterial treatise on ethics, *Reasons and Persons*, finds difference too slender a base on which to build a morality. Or, one might add, a politics. Among the categories conflated by the *pharmakos* is the Lacanian trinity of imaginary, symbolic and Real. In so far as this beast is a fearful double, both stranger and brother, alien and ally, it belongs in Lacanian idiom to the sphere of the imaginary; but it is also an emanation of the Real, one with the power to rupture and remake the symbolic order.

Schopenhauer writes of the individual who no longer makes a distinction between himself and others, but 'must regard the endless suffering of all that lives as his own, and take upon himself the pain of the whole world'.[3] A minor example of this selfless indifference is the saintly Denis Nolan of Iris Murdoch's *The Unicorn*, who removes himself from the house in which the novel is set in order to purge it of a pervasive violence. One thinks also of Francis Stuart's strange, compelling, idiosyncratic novel *Redemption*. Towards the end of the nineteenth century, it is the artist above all who comes to stand for this empathy with the afflictions of others, sacrificing his or her individual fulfilment for the sake of sympathetically recreating the sufferings of others. Those who seek perfection of the work must forgo perfection of the life, plunging into the depths of human depravity in order to transmute it into something rich and rare. A somewhat parodic version of this 'infinitely gentle, infinitely suffering thing', to quote T.S. Eliot, crops up in August Strindberg's play *Easter*, in which Eleonora Heyst indulges a morbid impulse to take upon herself the burden of other people's pain.

The idea of the scapegoat also exerts a compelling force over one of the finest critical minds of the modern age. Commenting on William Empson's *Some Versions of Pastoral*, John Haffenden writes that

the pastoral hero is discovered to be at once the representative figure and the exceptional one (macrocosm and microcosm, complex and simple): he is at once the Many in so far as he embodies all and everything, and also the One as he comprehends all and everything: he is both insider and outsider, all-inclusive and emblematic.[4]

Empson connects the scapegoat with both the artist and the criminal, as a figure who is outside society because he is too poor to benefit from it, but who in his consequent independence can act as a judge or critic of the social order that judges him. If the scapegoat is a sympathetic criminal, Empson adds, he can be made to suggest both Christ and the sacrificial tragic hero.[5] Like the sacrificial victim, the scapegoat embraces negativity in the name of a greater good.

The ancient scapegoat is an 'objective' version of such self-sacrifice, one which has not yet been cranked up a gear to moral consciousness. As a metaphorical figure standing in for others, it involves a short circuit between universal and individual. Precisely because it is nothing in itself, the scapegoat has the ability to represent the community as a whole; and since this capacity of a single figure to incarnate the whole is also true of the king or chieftain, the lowliest of creatures has a resonance of the highest. As we have seen already in the case of Marx, the status of scapegoat will be inherited in modern times by the revolutionary subject. Like that subject, the scapegoat bears witness in its tainted flesh to the obscene underside of the social order, marking the place where its hidden antagonisms come to light. As such, it signifies an exclusion which maintains the polis in being but which dare not speak its name. It is the nearest civilisation can approach to producing a palpable image of the violence that is one of its enabling conditions. And since only those who embody social contradictions are able to transform them, the very frailty of this outcast is a sign of its potential strength. It is this ambivalence of power and weakness that the idea of the *pharmakos* seeks to capture. In ancient Greek mythology, it is the one whose wounded foot leaks stinking pus who wields the bow that can save the city.

There are those who are victimised because they are thought to be befouled, but the ancient scapegoat is befouled because it is a victim. The less blemished its own existence, the clearer becomes its representative status – the fact that it acts on behalf of others, whose corruption then stands out all the more starkly against the backdrop of its own blamelessness. To be sacred means to be set apart, but not

146

necessarily set above. As with the *anawim*, the poor and powerless of the Hebrew Scriptures, it can be a matter of being set below. The destitute have nothing but God, which is one reason why they are holy. Indeed, it is because they have nothing of their own that they can bear the most eloquent witness to Yahweh's transfigurative power. We bear our treasure in earthen vessels, St Paul observes in his Second Letter to the Corinthians, to testify to the truth that it springs from a source beyond ourselves.

Rather as in baptism the subject freely assumes a guilt for which she is not personally responsible (so-called original sin), thus rehearsing Christ's action on the cross, so the flesh of the *pharmakos* soaks up the collective guilt of the polis. As René Girard remarks, the purpose of this figure is 'to literally draw to himself all the infectious strains in the community and transform them into sources of peace and fecundity.'[6] Only by becoming a living image of vice can it restore virtue. As the Duke remarks in *Measure for Measure*, 'there is so great a fever on goodness that the dissolution of it must cure it' (Act III Scene 2). For this purpose, the scapegoat combines more or less the whole range of Freudian mechanisms: condensation, displacement, projection, doubling, substitution, transference, disavowal and the like. As a lowly bit of matter invested with universal meaning, a profane piece of flesh bathed in a numinous aura, it is a symbol par excellence. It is granted both the reverence and the animosity due to all things that are terrible to look on. As both revered and reviled, it is what has been called a guilty innocent.

For Aristotle, the tragic hero is not exactly blessed with the innocence of the scapegoat; but nor is he wholly culpable, for if he were he would fail to evoke the pity and sympathy of the spectators. Yet

Oedipus, a *pharmakos* who is both poison and cure, man and monster, stranger and brother, hunter and prey, husband and son, insider and outsider, lawgiver and outlaw, king and beggar, all and nothing, is neither guilty nor innocent but a guilty innocent. The guilty innocent may also be a raped woman like Samuel Richardson's Clarissa, objectively chaste but subjectively sullied. As Jacques Derrida writes in *Dissemination*, the *pharmakos* 'represents evil both introjected and projected. Beneficial insofar as he cures – and for that, venerated and cared for – harmful insofar as he incarnates the powers of evil – and for that, feared and treated with caution. Alarming and calming. Sacred and accursed.'[7] The truly sacred creature, which is to say the one who is inseparably cursed and blessed, is none other than humanity itself, the Sphinx-like conundrum that pitches moral distinctions into disarray as surely as the infected, immaculate scapegoat. Humanity – an amalgam of sovereign and beast, supra-human and subhuman – is the monster that should be treated with pity, but also with fear.

The structure of scapegoating is metaphorical. In an act of collective transference, the *pharmakos* stands in for the people as a whole, who by thrusting it into the desert or beyond the city walls ritually disavow their own iniquities. In expelling this outsider, they also mark out their own political terrain. A rigorous distinction between purity and pollution is thus enforced, one which the ambiguously holy and defiled *pharmakos* itself throws into question. James George Frazer believes that an inability to distinguish between holiness and pollution is a distinctive feature of 'primitive' thought. To make such a distinction, claims William Robertson Smith, 'marks a real advance above savagery'.[8] Neither scholar would presumably have been much taken with St Paul's Letter to the Romans, which regards the distinction between the clean and unclean as having been abolished by the death and resurrection of Christ. Notions of purity and defilement are consigned to the paranoid past, to be replaced by a contrast between grace and sin – which is to say, roughly speaking, between a profusion of life and a deficiency of it.

To disown the *pharmakos* is to identify with it in the very act of rejecting it, in a 'this is us, but not us' ambiguity. As in the Lacanian imaginary, there is both mimesis and antagonism, identity and estrangement. Frazer maintains that the custom of scapegoating arises from the crass literalisation of a metaphor, one which takes as a material fact the transferring of one's ailments to another. It is, he considers, a 'pathetic fallacy' typical of the 'cunning and selfish savage'.[9] Even so, the strategy is still widespread in our own post-barbaric times. One might glimpse an improbable descendant of the *pharmakos* in the figure of the psychoanalyst, who likewise becomes the focus of illicit impulses, and whose dissolution of this transference at a key point in the therapy may be seen as a remote equivalent to packing the scapegoat off into the desert.

The alternative way of treating the scapegoat is as metonymic, acknowledging this thing of darkness as one's own or as a part of oneself. In the act traditionally known as repentance, one finds in this frightfully disnatured apparition, this holy terror at one's gates, an image of the death-dealing, life-giving Real which the community must confront if it is to be redeemed.[10] What the polis sees in this abject creature is not simply what it has cast out as so much waste produce, but the deformity that this act of expulsion has inflicted upon itself. In beholding this sign of its own monstrosity, it acknowledges that to take the scapegoat in will involve metanoia, or fundamental self-renewal. It is not simply a matter of extending its frontiers. Giorgio Agamben strikes the keynote when he remarks, 'that which is excluded from the community is, in reality, that on which the entire life of the community is founded'.[11] As such, its reincorporation is bound to shake the social order to its foundations, in contrast to some banal postmodern gesture of 'inclusivity'.

Sympathy with the scapegoat is neither the magical affinity of mimesis nor the narcissism of the imaginary. It is rather a question of solidarity with the dereliction it signifies. *Agape*, writes Jürgen Moltmann, is 'love of the non-existent, love of the unlike, the unworthy, the worthless, of the lost, the transient and the dead'.[12] As in the state Freud calls the uncanny, this loathsome being is at once foreign and familiar. In order to embrace it, terror must be transmuted into pity. In an interplay of intimacy and otherness, we are required to permutate the two standard Aristotelian responses to tragedy and feel sympathy for what we fear. In coming to feel for it in its very monstrosity, the imaginary domain, in which the other is at once rival and alter ego, can be converted into a more fruitful interplay of difference and identity, this time in the register of the Real.

In metaphorical or surrogate scapegoating, the community draws strength from the victim's weakness; in the metonymic mode, its power lies in confessing its own infirmity, recognising in the scapegoat an image of its own criminality. To treat the beast in this manner is to root the symbolic in the Real, grounding the social order in what threatens to bring it to ruin. The slogan of metonymic scapegoating is not 'this is us, but not us', but 'this is more myself than I am, that in me which is more than me'. It is this, traditionally, that is claimed by the human subject not simply of the scapegoat but of God. In the mirror of God's sublimely fearful otherness, the subject is able to glimpse something of its own infinity, while in the mirror of the *pharmakos* it can grasp an image of its own nullity. Yet the close affiliation of nullity and infinity is a familiar feature of the sublime, which on the one hand raises us to vertiginous heights, but on the other hand, by showing up our puniness against the background of its own boundlessness, plunges us into abysmal depths. It is a duality equally true of the scapegoat, a living icon of powerlessness who can thereby prove a redemptive force. As in so much tragic art, only the fertile dissolution of non-being can reclaim powers oblivious of their own finitude.

Psychoanalytically speaking, the act of disavowal involves both spurning and preserving, and this is also true of the scapegoat. The polis may be keen to cast this rough beast out, but it also wants to assimilate something of its uncanny power, one rendered all the more efficacious by its being thrust into the ambiguously death-dealing, life-giving borderlands of the political order. The sacred is that which is dangerous, abandoned, lost, redemptive, cursed, excluded, holy, transformative and unclean. As such, the concept seeks to come to terms with the fact that humanity's creative powers are closely entwined with its urge to lay waste. What one must do, then, is shield one's eyes from the terror of the sacred while at the same time tapping into its formidably restorative power. In a Badiou-like event, Theseus, ruler of Athens, endangers the well-being of his people by gathering the stinking piece of matter known as Oedipus to the heart of the polis, in the faith that a formidable power for good may flow from this audacious act of hospitality. To welcome into the city those who incarnate the ruins and remnants of humanity is to risk a general desecration; but to be courageous enough to do so is to be rewarded with a miraculous renewal of life. 'I come to offer you a gift – my tortured body – a sorry sight', the blind self-exile cries in *Oedipus at Colonus*, 'but there is value in it more than beauty'. 'The very excess of [Oedipus's] defilement', writes Jean-Pierre Vernant, 'qualifies him to be the tutelary hero of Athens.'[13] So it is that Oedipus the monster becomes Oedipus the divine. 'Surely some god will raise him up!' chants the Chorus.

When it comes to this Janus-faced creature, then, Keats's renowned dictum proves to be false. It is ugliness that is truth, not beauty. The repulsiveness of the scapegoat distils something of the horror of the human condition, but in doing so can give birth to acts of great moral splendour. In some African societies, Mary Douglas writes, 'a hybrid monster, which in secular life one would expect them to abhor, is reverently eaten by initiates and taken to be the most powerful source of fertility ... That which is rejected is ploughed back for a renewal of life.'[14] In similar vein, St Paul writes in his First Letter to the Corinthians that God 'chose what is foolish in the world to shame the wise; God chose what is weak in the world to shame the strong; God chose what is low and despised in the world, things that are not, to reduce to nothing things that are' (1 Corinthians 1:27–8). It is pure negativity that will confound the powers of this world, who even now, Paul grimly adds, 'are coming to nothing'. Indeed, the whole of his work can be read as a meditation on the paradoxes of frailty and power – of how Yahweh, lord of the carnivalesque, has brought low the wisdom of the theorists and ideologues by raising up those who, like the apostle himself, are 'fools for

Christ's sake', having been made 'the shit of the earth, the off-scouring of all things' (1 Corinthians 4:13). As in the traditional act of sacrifice, the world is undergoing a momentous transition from weakness to power – a passage of which the sacred, self-contradictory, cursed-and-blessed state of the powerless is the sign.

The Christian version of this transition is centred on the Eucharist. The death re-enacted by the ritual is also the ground of a new form of friendship. The Eucharist is a love feast, but one based on the symbolic consuming of a polluted body. It is an act of solidarity established by participating in the passage of a destitute creature from failure to flourishing, so that at the root of this comradeship lies a form of monstrosity. An abject piece of matter is gathered up into the praxis of a shared meal. The traumatic kernel of the Real is inserted into the symbolic order in order to reconfigure it.[15] That which was rejected as unclean is ploughed back for a renewal of human life. The non-being of the outcast becomes the cornerstone of a new form of communality. The violence associated with sacrifice is no longer that of the powers that establish the social order in the first place, but the virulent aggression inflicted by that authority on those like Jesus who speak out for a different conception of human solidarity. In commemorating a revolutionary Passover from death to life, turning back to the site of the primordial trespass, the Eucharist brings that saving event to bear on the present as the promise of an emancipated future.

It is a disruption of secular time that lies at the very heart of the idea of the sacred. As Edmund Leach argues of pre-modern cultures, social existence comes to appear discontinuous 'by inserting intervals of liminal, sacred non-time into the continuous flow of normal secular time.'[16] In commemorating the death of Christ, the Eucharist breaks into the continuum of history, bringing it to a momentary standstill, short-circuiting time by abbreviating past, present and future in a single memorable icon or dialectical image. Like Benjamin's 'angel of history', it turns its eyes to a lethal past in an act of revolutionary remembrance, in order to permit the transformative force of that trauma to impel it into the future. In doing so, it brings the uncanny power of the living dead to bear on the deathly condition of the living. As Freud warns, those who do not truly remember are condemned to repeat, as with the compulsive repetition of ritual sacrifice.

* * *

The *pharmakos* in classical antiquity was usually human – a prisoner or citizen down on his luck who was hired, housed and paid to participate in certain purgative rituals. The original scapegoat of the Book of Leviticus, however, is an animal – one whose literally non-human status can be seen to signify the moral inhumanity it represents. As a figure that hovers undecidably between life and death, it is reminiscent of Giorgio Agamben's robotic Muselmann, the concentration camp victim whose existence is a species of living death, and who as a chilling signifier of the Real has in Primo Levi's words stared the Gorgon in the face. As with the ancient scapegoat, the Muselmann's disfigured humanity is an image of the crimes of his oppressors. At the heart of Nazism lay a kind of living death.[17] According to his doctor, Hitler spent his last days like a barely animated corpse. A similar example of such a figure can be found in old Fouan, the avaricious peasant of Émile Zola's *The Earth*, who is finally reduced to a state of almost pure animality. The Muselmann, Agamben writes, is the site where humanity itself is called into question. He is the human being who, like Oedipus or Lear, has survived the human being.[18] Yet so too, Agamben would wish to claim, are all humans.

The Muselmann lacks the ancient scapegoat's redemptive capacity. The horror of power is not here counterpointed by the power of horror. There is death, but no resurrection. This ravaged creature is not even tragic, at least in the classical sense of a protagonist raised by his death to sublime status. Instead, we have entered upon the Beckettian realm of the post-tragic, in which the very idea that suffering could have a meaning seems either risible or obscene. The broken, scooped-out subjects of this world are no longer even capable of the degree of meaning that might qualify them as candidates for tragedy. Agency itself is quite beyond them. All the same, there is a ghastly kind of value to be glimpsed even in these derelict figures. If the Muselmann incarnates the malevolence of power, he also represents its dead end – not only in the sense that any power prepared to take such measures is spiritually bankrupt, but also because it can exert no hold over those who are blankly indifferent to its authority. Those who can fall no further are strangely invulnerable. You cannot murder the dead. 'Nothing can save the conquered but the knowledge that they cannot now be saved', cries Virgil's Aeneas, urging his soldiers to fight on even though Troy is doomed. *Homo sacer* has died to himself, and so can be neither robbed nor mocked, spurned nor shamed, violated nor humiliated. The body of the beggarman is thus imbued with something of the inviolability of the person of the king. At this degree-zero of humanity, the destitute represent a gruesome, cruelly parodic image of the dominant. Because they have no investment in the status quo, such figures have nothing left to lose, which is why they emanate the aura of danger typical of all sacred powers. An effective despot must subjugate his victims, but not to the point where he can no longer solicit their active submission. Power seeks recognition, and is gravely disabled without it. The Muselmann, it is true, is not out to challenge power, but he embraces it no more than the dissident does. Power itself has set him free of itself. In this sense, too, the inhuman is blessed as well as cursed.

The Muselmann offers men and women an icon of their own inhumanity, without a confession of which there would be no possibility of redemption. As a sign of the fathomless nature of human depravity, he also indicates how deep-seated the cure for it would have to be. This is one of several senses in which this accursed figure is also strangely blessed. He is a sign of sheer, unadorned humanity, the poor forked creature of Shakespeare's *King Lear*, terrible to look on since stripped of all decorous cultural drapery. As such, he is a memento of what any politically transformative project must take as its foundation if it is to hold firm. The eviscerated creature of the camps represents the paradox that when we are stripped of our cultural lendings, hacked down to bare life, we are at our least and most human. Least human, because culture is constitutive of our humanity; most human, because those plundered of their cultural identities have no claim on their fellows but a human or universal one. If the Muselmann is the very prototype of the human, it is not least because for psychoanalytic thought the human subject itself emerges only through a traumatic encounter with the death-dealing

Real, one which divests it of its substance. We have all, so to speak, survived one death already – a condition of which the Muselmann, who has survived yet another and whose body lives on to tell the tale, is exemplary. It is in this absolute, culturally unmarked demand of *homo sacer*, a figure without an essence, that the essence of humanity is established, deeper than all difference. There is also a sense in which the compassion that this figure evokes must itself be inhuman. Only an impersonal (which is to say, political or institutional) love could repair this calamity, one based not upon sentiment but upon practice, not on the friend but on the stranger, not on the symbolic but on the Real.

'Am I now a man', cries the blind, beggarly Oedipus, 'only when I am no longer human?' The Muselmann, who inhabits that hellish region beyond all articulate meaning known to the ancient Greeks as *ate*, is a sign of inhumanity not only because he is the hapless victim of cruelty. He is also a reminder of the loss of humanity to which we are all headed. Bare life means among other things that any human existence is constituted in part by its capacity to be cut off. Among the most radical forms of equality is our common killability. 'Destructibility', writes Walter Benjamin, 'is the bond that unites in harmony everything that exists.'[19] As potential *homines sacri*, our common susceptibility to political murder constitutes a potent egalitarian bond. It is on this demonic truth, rather than some angelic dream of utopia, that a more-than-imaginary community might be built. A positive form of de-differentiation, one that acknowledges that individuals are alike in their being-towards-death and political vulnerability, must be distinguished from a murderous disregard for individual difference.

A capacity for the loss of humanity, then, is constitutive of humanity. Indeed, it represents its ultimate possibility. The human as fact can be stripped of the human as value – not in the sense that men and women cease to be human when they are treated like garbage, but in the sense that their existence may cease to make sense. To be dehumanised is a peculiar mark of the human species, and the Muselmann is a prototype of humanity in just this sense. It is not simply that he remains human in his dehumanisation; it is rather that, as we have seen already, he is at his most human in this devastated condition. 'The human being', writes Agamben, 'is the inhuman; the one whose humanity is completely destroyed is the one who is truly human.'[20] In death, this is true in a literal sense. Being able to reflect on their mortality sets men and women apart from the other animals, but at the same time intensifies their sense of creatureliness, thus making them more rather than less animal than their fellow beasts.[21] Yet whereas non-human animals are unable to shed their animal identities, just such a divestment is of the nature of human drive and desire, as opposed to the innocent creatureliness of instinct. The drive for Freud represents an aberration from our animal existence, rather as desire signifies a momentous disruption of it, pitching it dramatically out of kilter.

There are other senses in which the Muselmann's inhumanity is an index of the human. It is not only that he thereby manifests a barbarism endemic to the species, but that he signifies how being human is a matter of material fact, and as such represents the ruin of all high-minded cultural idealism. It is out of material, 'inhuman' or impersonal phenomena (being, Nature, language, desire, *thanatos*, kinship, economies, institutions, codes and conventions, the materiality of the flesh and so on) that human subjects are manufactured, which is not to say that they are reducible to such constituents. Only by acknowledging the anonymous material infrastructure of their being can they hope to transcend it. Yet there is also a darker meaning to Agamben's comment in *Remnants of Auschwitz* that 'Humans bear within themselves the mark of the inhuman.'[22] It is also true in the sense that anybody, including those who may later be reduced to the condition of the Muselmann, is capable of exterminating anyone else. This, too, is part of the way we bear mortality along with us.

The Muselmann, having died as a moral agent, lives on as a human organism. He is not a moral being in himself, simply in what he signifies for others. Yet there is a positive as well as a negative aspect to his survival. What this eviscerated creature has lost is not only the power to love, feel and act purposefully, but the capacity to do to others what has been done to him. That he cannot return evil for evil is in his case not a question of value but a matter of fact. As one who has passed beyond the horizon of the ethical, he is in this sense without blame, rather like the ancient scapegoat. If he is cursed in his disfigured humanity, he is blessed in this respect. Those who are without power are unable to maim and abuse, rather as those without material goods are free of the vices of those overburdened with them. In this sense, the oppressed and exploited are marked by what one might call a social or objective rather than individual or subjective innocence. They, too, are guilty innocents, blameless of the crimes of which they remain a stark embodiment.

For Christian faith, God is present most fundamentally in the dispossessed. Their loss of humanity reflects his own non-human otherness, as well as the terrifyingly inhuman nature of his unconditional love. The poor are signs of Yahweh in the fact that they are dependent on him alone, having been abandoned by all human powers. Yet if they are negative images of his kingdom, it is also because by their mere existence they signify what is still politically to be done to help achieve it. They are a sign of the unfinished business of history, and in this sense testimony to what must still be accomplished. The only true image of the future is the failure of the present. By defining the limits of a social order, the excluded and rejected mark out the frontiers where it must exceed itself, so that surplus as waste can become surplus as transcendence. The transition from Christianity to Marxism is among other things one from a vision of the poor as prefiguring the future to a faith in them as the prime means of its attainment.

* * *

The Victorians could never decide whether children were angels or demons, unfallen creatures or the spawn of Satan. Romantics and Evangelicals joined battle over these amphibious creatures, at once alien and intimate. If there is something unsettling about children, as many a horror movie bears witness, it is because they are uncanny, being at once like their elders and not like them at all, pocket-size adults yet denizens of a different domain. And if children are marked in this way by the ambivalence of the scapegoat, they also fulfil something of its function. In the novels of Dickens, for example, the child figures often enough as a guilty innocent or (in Thomas Mann's phrase) holy sinner, one whose status as victim brings an entire oppressive order vividly into focus. In novels such as *Bleak House* and *Great Expectations*, there is a sense in which all adults in this irresponsible society have been cruelly orphaned. Dorothy Van Ghent speaks of the Dickensian child as one

> who must necessarily take upon himself responsibility not only for what is to be done in the present and the future, but what has been done in the past, inasmuch as the past is part and parcel of the present and the future. The child is the criminal, and it is for this reason that he is able to redeem his world.[23]

Half in and half out of the conventional social world, a dweller in civil society but not a participant in it, children are magnets for the obloquy and aggression of the ruling order. The infantile adults and prematurely aged children who throng Dickens's work are liminal creatures like the *pharmakos*, guiltless yet wretched, unworldly yet marked by signs of woe. Much the same is true of William Blake, for whom children can be either fiends or faultless victims.

Women, too, whom the Victorians frequently found hard to distinguish from children, can play the role of *pharmakoi*, being both pure and unregenerate. Like the child, they stand for the ambiguity of Nature itself, at once spiritual solace and red in tooth and claw, Rousseau and Darwin in the same body. The role of the woman as embodying a more pervasive social wrong is a prime concern of the Gothic novel. Yet from Cordelia and Miranda to Clarissa Harlowe and Clarissa Dalloway, female figures can also exercise a mysteriously redemptive power, which is less obviously true of the child. If the scapegoat is both poison and cure, an image of the corrupt present but also an agent of its transformation, the child, *pace* Van

Ghent, is more the site of a problem than the sign of a solution. The blamelessness that makes it an unwitting indictment of a brutal society also prevents it from grasping the sources of that violence, and thus how it might be changed.

* * *

Because the scapegoat is burdened with the sins of many men and women, it is a hybrid, composite beast, and as such a sort of monster. The monster is traditionally a patchworked creature, made like the Sphinx out of heterogeneous bits and pieces. Confronted with this exotic amalgam, it is impossible, as it is with humanity itself, to return a simple answer to the question 'What is it?', as the riddle of the Sphinx makes clear. Its multiplicity belongs with its impurity, as well as with its grotesqueness; but the same misshapenness can be a virtue, allowing a single creature to blend, say, the intellect of a man with the strength of a lion. Power and impurity are thus strangely akin. They are also at one in the fact that the more multifarious the scapegoat is, given the variety of trespasses it bears on its back, the more all-encompassing grows its salvific power. Any creature capable of redeeming such a diverse condition will need to be thoroughly mongrelised. As a dappled, brindled beast, the monster confounds features which ought to be distinguished, pitching them together in a way offensive to both social order and aesthetic symmetry. It scrambles differences and plays havoc with hierarchies. As such, it looms up as a frightful version of carnival, but also as the very image of heteroclite, self-divided, miscegenated humanity. It is a kind of liminal state incarnate, and liminal states are considered by much pre-modern thought to be peculiarly dangerous.

Oedipus Tyrannus broods on these paradoxes of unity and plurality, conundrums which come to a head in the question of incest. Incest is the condition in which roles are illicitly merged and vital distinctions eroded. Like the riddle of the Sphinx, it can also conflate different generations into one. Both incest and parricide, in Malcolm Bull's term, are 'difference-dissolving'. Incest, the very type of human monstrosity, treats those who should be other as intimate – a condition which, as with Oedipus, can then render you a stranger to yourself, abolishing the otherness that is a condition of authentic selfhood. As such, this fearful aberration lays bare the truth of the human condition, in which we are in any case enigmas to ourselves, bearing at the core of our being a fearful Real which, like God for Augustine and Aquinas, is closer to us than we are to ourselves. In its interplay of the familiar and outlandish, then, incest has an affinity with the scapegoat. Both incest and monstrosity throw crucial discriminations into disarray, and in doing so make a carnivalesque mockery of the symbolic order. At the same time, however, they can be seen as an image of that order itself, once it is viewed not as a stable system of roles but as the untotalisable text of the Other – as a skein of tightly knotted motives, actions, effects and identities which can never be fully unravelled into their distinctive strands.

Since garblings and levellings are of the nature of *eros*, which is no respecter of rank, gender or ethnicity, and since the perverse permutations of incest are an essential possibility of any fully operative symbolic order, a certain monstrosity is installed at the very heart of the polis. It is a condition of social roles being combined correctly that they can always be combined inappropriately. Deviations are thus as much the product of norms as transgressions are of law.

It is by coming to recognise this Real at the core of the symbolic, which is also the impenetrable riddle of individual identity, that Oedipus can be redeemed. He must come to acknowledge that in the tangled web of the Other, or social unconscious, for which one ancient name is Fate, no individual can assuredly call his act or self-hood his own.

If there is an inherent impropriety about *eros*, so is there about death. Death, too, is a leveller which respects no differences. It is as ruthlessly indiscriminate as desire. The orgy and the act of genocide are alike indifferent to the particularity of human bodies. In striking all odds even, death smacks of political subversion. It also allows us to view any particular social regime *sub specie aeternitatis*, thus unmasking its absolutist pretensions. This is one sense in which seeking to anticipate one's death can pose a threat to the ruling order. Death and monstrosity are akin in exposing the provisional nature of social forms, thus making for a certain constructive detachment from them. Both Marxism and Christianity practise a form of irony in this respect, engaging in the actual yet also grasping it in the light of its passing away. Mary Douglas writes of those African cults which embrace the monstrous and hybrid that 'by the mystery of that rite [the participants] recognise something of the fortuitous and conventional nature of the categories in whose mould they have their experience'.[24] Rather as the monster is a hotchpotch of scraps and leavings, so an encounter with it can breed a sense of alternative possibilities, highlighting the arbitrary nature of social orthodoxy and illuminating the limits of its sway. What marks off this sense of other possibilities from some callow postmodern cult of options or supermarket of the soul is its tragic structure. The encounter with the monster is a question of trauma, self-dispossession and self-remaking – which is to say, in theological terms, of repentance and conversion. *Pace* the postmodernists, hybridity is not always to be commended. The composite nature of the scapegoat is a demonic rather than angelic version of it. Postmodernism celebrates the hybrid but tends to defuse its horror. It fails to recognise that there are repugnant forms of plurality (a plurality of fascist states, for example) and injurious modes of transgression, as well as situations that demand solidarity rather than heterogeneity. It was not through a celebration of difference that South African apartheid or the neo-Stalinist bureaucracies were brought to their knees. There are also distinctions (between racism and non-racism, for example) that need to be enforced rather than annulled. Demarcations can help to stem a strain of indiscriminate violence. When the hybrid is pressed to the point where differences are simply confounded, the result can be calamitous, as in the holy terror of the Dionysian. Marx viewed capitalism, a form of life on which he lavished praise as well as condemnation, as a monstrous form of existence. It was the most promiscuous regime known to human history, boundless and malformed, a freakish medley of different life forms and a stranger to all measure or proportion. Its constant transgression of boundaries was in one sense exhilarating and in another sense alarming. And if the pied and dappled are not always to be applauded, neither is all hierarchy to be scorned as unsound. The individual who does not cherish some features of the world more than others is yet to see the light of day. The point is not to flatten distinctions in some ultra-leftist fervour, but to acknowledge the precariousness of such differences while continuing to hold fast to their necessity. This, too, involves a certain ironic mode of living.

The problem is how to dismantle the more repressive forms of order and hierarchy without reducing everything to the sameness of shit. How is a creative form of hybridity to be kept from sliding into the slime, dust, mud and sludge which lurk at the root of social existence in the later Dickens? How is one to draw a line between a precious kind of piedness and the purely amorphous? Hell is sometimes portrayed as a place of absolute self-identity, one with the endless uniformity of excrement. There is a vein of tragic art for which one has to be hauled through this desert of the Real in order to recognise the arbitrariness of one's previous scale of values, and so to emerge with some more authentic view of what is to be prized. The cynic or nihilist, by contrast, is one who folds death back into life, allowing the prospect of the end of value to sabotage the current reality of it. In this sense, he differs from those for whom death puts value in perspective rather than undercutting it, finding in it an egalitarian spirit capable of questioning the more specious calibrations of the present. It is one of the most enduring forms of egalitarianism, as well as of solidarity. In death, as in the *pharmakos*, men and women can discover some kinship, and have a chance to reconstruct the polis in the light of this fact.

In Mary Douglas's classic study *Purity and Danger*, the role of the scapegoat or monster in pre-modern cultures is played by dirt, which is essentially matter out of place. Dirt in Douglas's view is a kind of anomaly or ambiguity, a blurring of precise categories which involves 'reflection on the relation of order to disorder, form to formlessness, life to death'.[25] It signifies the fortuitous nature of social systems, but can also be taken to represent their least privileged members. Where there is dirt there is system, since dirt is system's waste product. A virtue of Douglas's study, however, is that it does not set system and its surplus against each other in some simple-minded polarity. It thus avoids one of the major blunders of post-structuralism, one glaringly apparent in the work of the later Derrida, for which system, norm, law, doctrine, programme, convention, institution and consensus are covertly demonised, while whatever they cannot contain is indiscriminately commended. In our own time, this has been a distinctively Gallic intellectual vice, one also to be found in Alain Badiou's otherwise suggestive antithesis between being and void, as well as in Jacques Rancière's distinction between politics and the police. It is a duality everywhere apparent in the writings of Gilles Deleuze and Félix Guattari. For a disenchanted cohort writing in the wake of 1968, virtue can now be found only in the margins and fissures of the political system – in forces that momentarily disrupt it, or in the shape of an event which bursts miraculously through its oppressive logic. At worst, there can be no positive system, any more than there can be an illicit transgression. Sporadic dissent is preferable to organised resistance. 'Marginal', a category that includes both neo-Nazis and Rosicrucians, becomes ipso facto affirmative. In its denigration of the regulated, conventional sphere of everyday existence – a disdain scarcely surprising in intellectuals who are personally remote from it – it represents a secular version of the Protestant split between grace and Nature.

Douglas, despite her conservative Roman Catholic legacy, is guilty of no such lapse. Indeed, her Catholicism has the advantage of alerting her to the ineradicably institutional nature of social existence. If the waste product that falls outside a regime is a manifestation of the sacred, so too are the forces that make for social order. As

Giorgio Agamben remarks, 'both the law and he who violates it are sacred'.[26] Those who flout the Law become sacred by virtue of their abrasive contact with it. Disorder, which in Douglas's phrase is a kind of 'creative formlessness', spoils pattern, but also provides the material for a new configuration. The sacred is thus politically double-edged. It both sustains and subverts. A negative version of this ambiguity can be found in the Old Testament image of Satan. On the one hand, the name 'Satan' denotes a false, despotic social order. As prince of darkness, the devil is a type of the 'rulers and authorities' whom Paul in Colossians sees as having in principle been brought to their knees by the resurrection of Jesus. On the other hand, Satan is a veritable 'dragon of chaos', a source of nihilism and fount of pure futility hostile to the very idea of order and meaning.

In Douglas's view, the perilous powers that lurk on the edges of the social system can renew as well as destroy it. There is a fruitful dialectic at work between social order and its human detritus. Slavoj Žižek reminds us that 'at the very core of Christianity . . . there is a destructive negativity which ends not in a chaotic Void, but reverts (and organises itself) into a new Order'.[27] René Girard speaks of the monster or scapegoat as 'a result of decomposition followed by a recombination'.[28] The monster dissolves the given order, but in doing so clears the ground for it to be reconstructed. It is sacred because it lurks on the periphery of the social order, but also because it contains the capacity to transform it. Indeed, there is a sense in which the act of excluding this rough beast is itself sacred, since it is what founds the community in the first place. It signifies the primordial sacrifice that brings the world into being. At the same time, what is banished by this original act also has a prodigiously fertile power.

The ambiguity of the term 'sacred' marks an attempt to grapple with this contradiction.

Julia Kristeva's comments on Mary Douglas's work in *Powers of Horror* are typical of a failure to do so.[29] In predictable post-structuralist style, Kristeva sees dirt simply in terms of exclusion, not as a force for reconstruction. It is subversive but not transformative. The idea of order as such is implicitly denigrated, while the forces of anarchy and disruption are uncritically affirmed. Yet one does not subvert a set-up merely by a sentimental embrace of whatever it happens to reject. That social order can foster and protect human life, as well as stifle and suppress it, is not a truth that post-structuralism is in general eager to acknowledge. Nor does it consort easily with Jacques Rancière's terse dismissal of the business of sustaining social existence as 'the politics of the police.'[30] In all such formulations, the striking ambiguity of the sacred is overlooked. Besides, in her somewhat cerebral relish for dirt and disorder, Kristeva sets aside the fact that there are abominations (rape, paedophilia and the like) which need to be banished, by force if necessary, from any human system. Not all inclusiveness is angelic. Exclusiveness, too, can be a virtue.

In an argument rather similar to Douglas's, Malcolm Bull maintains that apocalyptic thought differs in important respects from the cult of sacrifice. Whereas sacrifice in Bull's view repeats the exclusion from society of the dirt-like or undifferentiated, apocalypse includes what has been expelled in a way that fashions a new form of order, one less narrowly defined than before. 'Apocalyptic texts', Bull comments, 'often describe a process in which undifferentiated chaos is the prelude to a new order.'[31] One thinks of Yeats's rough beast, a creature who is to be feared as heralding the violent crack-up of the current historical cycle but welcomed as the harbinger of a new, heroic epoch. Apocalyptic doom is accordingly blended with eschatological hope. The chaos of the collapse of one regime is an essential prelude to the birth of its successor.

How should one deal with the forces of disorder? One can forcibly banish such anomalies, as Pentheus seeks disastrously to do with Dionysus in Euripides' *The Bacchae*; or one can contain their subversive force by granting them an honoured place within the polis. Aeschylus's Furies and Sophocles' Oedipus become resident aliens in the city, their destructive powers (*thanatos*) sublimated and institutionalised, turned outward in defence of the polis and as such pressed into the service of *eros*, builder of cities. As Girard comments, 'The greatest of all delinquents is transformed into a pillar of society.'[32] Alternatively, one can acknowledge that to incorporate what is cast out demands a deep-seated transformation of the existing structure, not simply a refurbishing of it. It is not just a question of renewing its vigour and bolstering its power. It is rather a matter of dismantling and reinventing, and thus of keeping faith with the ambiguous logic of the scapegoat.

*   *   *

If the powers that constitute the social order are sacred, as well as those that threaten to undermine it, it is hardly surprising that there should be a secret, handy-dandyish kinship between the king and the beggarman. In the ancient world, the *pharmakos* was often enough accorded the status of nobility because of the value it brought to the city.[33] The status of the ruler is in some ways akin to that of the outcast, so that Hobbes can write in *Leviathian* of the sovereign as a figure excluded from the community as a whole. For Giorgio Agamben, sovereign and *homo sacer* are curiously symmetrical figures. All men and women are potential *homines sacri* with respect to the ruler, while *homo sacer* is a figure with respect to whom all others can exert power. The kinship between sovereign and scapegoat is a familiar motif of social and religious thought in classical antiquity.[34] When the king becomes a tyrant unrestrained by law, he is as anti-social as a wild beast.

There are several ways in which this alliance can be conceived. For one thing, neither the king nor the beggar can be adequately represented – the former rising above representation in his near-divinity, the latter falling below it in his negligibility. In the shadowy, lawless regions beyond the borders of society, gods and beasts mingle and interbreed, both in their different ways absolved from political authority.[35] For the Christian doctrine of Incarnation, God himself is an animal. The sovereign, like the gods, is above the reach of the law, while the dispossessed fall below it. For another thing, absolute power, as the sole donor of meaning in a world bleached of inherent value, can encounter nothing outside itself to confirm its own sovereignty, and is thus always at risk of imploding. As such, it becomes a mirror image of those it eviscerates. Kierkegaard speaks of the all-powerful subject as 'a king without a country', ruling over nothing.[36] Conversely, as in the case of Shakespeare's Barnardine, those who can fall no further acquire a dangerous degree of freedom, akin to the ascendancy of those who can rise no higher. Those who fly high, by contrast, have further to fall than the lowly and make more of a splash in doing so, which is one reason why they are prime candidates for tragedy. If there is something foolish about the king, there is a touch of wisdom about the Fool. If the monarch is a hybrid of man and deity, the *pharmakos* is an unholy mixture of human and beast. Both ruler and beggar are faceless, anonymous creatures – the former on account of his supra-individual function as a representative of the collective; the latter because he is ransacked of personal identity, a condition which can then lay the ground for an alternative form of political communality.

The king is a kind of fool because the eminent are invariably objects of envy and resentment, as well as being often enough blinded by their own privilege. Many a tribal ceremony involves the chief being beaten or even slain. The monarch is himself a scapegoat, and non-regal scapegoats were commonly substituted for him in tribal cultures. Jesus pinned to the cross is the king as fool, while the Fool in *King Lear* describes himself as 'Lear's shadow'. If the Fool is wiser than the foolish, it is because he is conscious of his own clownishness. In raising his idiocy to the second power, self-irony becomes his salvation. Mircea Eliade notes in his *History of Religious Ideas* how many mythological heroes are monstrous, lame, rapacious, one-eyed, androgynous, sexually aberrant, parricides, cross-dressers and the like. Such infirmities, as they were then considered, link the powerful to the powerless.

Both monarch and Fool are also creatures of whim – capricious figures licensed to sport and frolic. The sovereign can act as he pleases because of his pre-eminence, while the Fool can do as he likes because of his nullity. All and nothing are equally absolved from limitation. In one sense, the Fool is superior to the monarch, since to be aware of one's own nothingness is to have an identity of a kind, and thus to pull rank over those who deludedly believe themselves to be everything. As symbolic representatives of the community as a whole, both figures can infect and lay waste: the sovereign with his august authority, the Fool or beggar with his contagious negativity. They are mirror images of each other, too, in the fact that the weakness of the one acts as a foil to the puissance of the other. The lowly are in this sense unwitting testimony to the power of the mighty. Paul's First Letter to the Corinthians, by contrast, sees the impotence of the poor as a critique of power, not as a confirmation of it: 'God chose what is weak in the world to shame the strong. God chose what is low and despised in the world, even things that are not, to bring to nothing things that are' (1 Corinthians 1:27–8). His own strength, Paul confesses, lies in his feebleness, which allows the power of God to be more visibly manifested in him. In this respect, the weak constitute the most appropriate vessels for divinity. Conversely, power itself bears the marks of fragility, crippled as it is by its paranoid anxiety and implacable malice. If the *anawim* are loathed as well as despised by their masters, it is among other things because they remind them of their own spiritual vacuity. Without these contemptible creatures, they would have no one to rule over, and thus no authority; but what value is there in lording it over those you have reduced to so much dross?

The king both nurtures and destroys, rather as the scapegoat both pollutes and redeems. Both are thus objects of popular ambiguity. As far as the scapegoat goes, the general execration of one who incarnates disease and disorder is hard to distinguish from universal veneration, given that the same beast also promises a cure for this blighted condition. Conversely, the people's reverence for the chief as a principle of social stability is never far from a certain murderous resentment of his privilege. If the Law, like the monarch, is sacred, it is not least because it is both life-giving and death-dealing, a source of mortal violence as well as the bedrock of social existence. The Law itself is a kind of *pharmakos*, a fact that accounts among other things for St Paul's ambivalent attitude to it.

A vigilant authority needs to stand at some Archimedean point outside the order it regulates in order to oversee it effectively; but like the Duke in *Measure for Measure*, it thereby courts the danger of losing touch with the common people and bringing itself into disrepute. Its very effort to be dispassionate may spell its ruin. Hence the myriad fables of kings moving incognito among their subjects, as the law seeks to install itself on the inside of the sphere on which it passes judgement. If true power is to be hegemonic rather than coercive, the future monarch must sport for a while with Falstaff, while the sovereign must lend an ear to the jester. In the end, reason must subjugate the senses and law bridle the mob; but to do so without inciting revolt they must infiltrate them from the inside, as a fifth columnist in the enemy camp.

* * *

Absolute power is a kind of anarchist. Since there is nothing to restrain it, it represents the very essence of transgression. For Freud, the urge to order is secretly in love with chaos. Such power is not only lawless in itself, but tends to breed lawlessness by provoking political rebellion, rather as St Paul sees the Law as perversely inciting transgression. This anarchy then in turn triggers authoritarian repression, and so on in a stalled dialectic. As Claudio remarks in *Measure for Measure*, 'So every scope by the immoderate use /

Turns to restraint' (Act I Scene 2). Angelo in the same play moves in the opposite direction, turning at the sight of an alluring female face from icily dispassionate governor to frenzied lecher. If the Law is crazed with vindictive desire, a nihilist in preacher's garb, there is also that within desire that seeks its own obstruction. In both cases, ruler and transgressor maintain a secret pact. We have seen already that sovereign power is among other things a sublimated version of the violence that founds the state.

There is thus a covert alliance between what sustains the state and what lays siege to it. 'The terrorist and the policeman both come from the same basket', remarks a character in Joseph Conrad's *The Secret Agent*. Dionysus is both outlaw and divinity, id and superego. Hegel sees history as the work of heroic pioneers who are forced to flout the mores of their age, and who thus bear all the marks of the lawbreaker. Freud held much the same view, as does Fyodor Dostoevsky's Raskolnikov. Visionary and delinquent are hard to tell apart. Hero, criminal and avant-garde artist may inhabit the same body, as with Honoré de Balzac's Vautrin. There can be no clear distinction between these roles in bourgeois society, where transgression is the everyday norm. The upright burgher in the bosom of his family is also the lawless entrepreneur of the marketplace.

Both king and *pharmakos*, fused in the figure of Oedipus or Jesus, are burdened with responsibility for the collective well-being of the populace. Both figures are also simultaneously inside and outside the law. 'Like Oedipus', writes René Girard, 'the king is at once stranger and son, the most intimate of insiders and the most bizarre of outsiders; he is an exemplar of enormous tenderness and frightful savagery.'[37] As *tyrannus*, Sophocles' protagonist is one who reigns by his own authority rather than by legitimate succession, and in this sense, too, is both inside and outside the polis. Indeed, for Carl Schmitt's classic study *Political Theology*, this is the true condition of all governing powers, defined as they are by a decision about when to suspend the law which does not itself fall within the frame of legality.[38] On this view, the law is extrinsic to itself, its supreme authority coincident with a certain creative lawlessness. The original act of establishing the law cannot fall within the purview of the legality it brings to birth.

Impotence and sovereign power also converge in the figure of the hunger striker or suicide bomber, who exercises a divine power over himself by bringing himself to nothing. It is a parodic inversion of God's act of Creation. He who is prepared to kill himself, Krillov remarks in Dostoevsky's *The Devils*, becomes a god. The pinnacle of human power is the capacity to consign oneself to nothingness. The suicide bomber is priest and sacrificial offering in the same body. He is the inverted mirror image of the martyr, who sheds his blood for the sake of others rather than enlisting the blood of the innocent in his cause. What cannot be annihilated by sovereign authority is the will to annihilate yourself, which in the case of the crazed anarchist professor of *The Secret Agent* – a man who treads a hair-thin line between time and eternity, permanently wired up with a bomb and permanently prepared to detonate it – becomes the deepest, most delirious form of freedom. However depleted your existence, it is still possible to ensure that you die as devastatingly as possible. Those whose lives are unsung and inconspicuous may enlist themselves in the roll call of the legendary by making a lethal street theatre out of their end.

Because the scapegoat is nothing, a disposable piece of non-being, it has no distinctive features of its own and thus can easily pass over into the universal. As such, it can present itself as a rival to the global reach of sovereign power. To be nothing is to be nothing in particular, and thus to be potentially everything. 'In love', writes Slavoj Žižek, 'I am nothing, but as it were a Nothing aware of itself, a Nothing paradoxically made rich through the very awareness of its lack.'[39] He might have added that to acknowledge the self as nothing is to transcend the self-serving illusions of the ego in order to be open to the reality of other selves. It is thus that love can follow on the heels of a certain metaphorical death.

'When man decides, like Oedipus, to carry the inquiry into what he is as far as it can go', writes Jean-Pierre Vernant, 'he discovers himself to be enigmatic, without consistency, without any domain of his own or any fixed point of attachment, with no defined essence, oscillating between being the equal of the gods and the equal of nothing at all.'[40] As with a venerable sequence of tragic protagonists from Aeschylus to Arthur Miller, Oedipus refuses to back down from the question of his own identity. In his perverse, epistemo-philiac passion for the Real, a condition with the power to turn any tragic hero to stone, he presses his existence to an extreme limit, courts his own destruction and in doing so is divested of his humanity. Yet it is precisely on this account that he can be finally apotheosised.

All and nothing also converge in the sublime, in which the cowed subject is shattered and overwhelmed, its mortal limits thrown into stark relief, yet in its very capacity to confront this condition without being annihilated is exultantly aware of an unfathomable power within itself which is more than its equal. It is a rhythm repeated in some tragic art, as the mighty are brought low only to be raised up again, this time in full awareness of their own paucity. That which was too beggarly to be represented is now too exalted to be so. 'I must reduce myself to zero', remarks Gandhi. 'So long as a man does not of his own free will count himself last among his fellow creatures, there is no salvation for him.'[41] In this sense, sublimity is the appropriate register of the human subject, the amphibious creature who is both sovereign and slave, everything and nothing. It is this doubleness that the scapegoat incarnates. In the sublime, as in sacrifice, an abject object is metamorphosed by some alchemical power into an infinite subject. The beggarman is anointed king, and a traumatic loss of selfhood is thus richly recompensed.

* * *

If René Girard sees the scapegoat as a source of social unity, Karl Marx regards it as a revolutionary agent:

> A class must be formed with radical chains, a class in civil society that is not a class of civil society, a class that is the dissolution of all classes, a sphere of society having a universal character because its sufferings are universal, and claiming no particular right because no particular wrong but absolute wrong is inflicted on it; a sphere that can claim no traditional title but only a human one … a sphere, finally, that cannot emancipate itself without emancipating itself from all the other spheres of society, thereby emancipating them; a sphere, in short, that represents the complete loss of humanity and can only redeem itself through

the total redemption of humanity. This dissolution of society existing as a specific class is the proletariat.[42]

This class-that-is-not-a-class is a scandal to thought, as much a conundrum and enigma as the Sphinx. Like Agamben's Muselmann, it is stripped of all specificity, and so makes no claim but a human one. Like the sacrificial tribute, it signifies the gain of humanity through the loss of it. For Marx, the proletariat (or indeed, one might add, any such ambiguously positioned group or class) is the unassimilable element, askew to the logic which generates it, both being and dissolution of being, stumbling block and keystone, particular yet potentially universal, the joker in the pack or (in Lacanian parlance) the part which is no part, the source of civilisation yet one which falls outside its ruling terms of reference. The words of 'The Internationale' – 'We once were naught, we shall be all' – should be read as implying a causal relation between those two conditions, which is where they differ from a stereotypical tale of rags to riches. Because the poor have less of a stake in the status quo than the well heeled, they have less to lose from the impending upheaval which Marx calls communism and the Christian Gospel calls the kingdom of God, and are thus more likely to be open to its advent. Like the *pharmakos*, the proletariat is a homeopathic creature, symptom of sickness but promise of cure. Like any symbol, it is resonant of more than itself, proclaiming a more general emancipation in its own transition from weakness to power. The tragic protagonist of Calvary is another victim of absolute wrong who lays claim to no traditional title except a human one. It is because, like Marx's proletariat, he incarnates

179

a general criminality, 'made sin' in Pauline phrase, that he is able to redeem it.

There is an implicit contrast in Marx's early writings between the self-dispossession of the proletariat and the self-denial of the capitalist. The act of expropriating the bodily powers of others involves performing a similar operation on one's own. It is not simply that the oppressed are impoverished while their masters thrive. On the contrary, both parties are doomed for different reasons to be plundered of their sensuous corporeal wealth. Asceticism, Marx considers, is an integral part of a profit-driven social order. 'Self-denial, the denial of life and of all human needs', he writes in the *Economic and Philosophical Manuscripts,*

> is [bourgeois political economy's] principal doctrine. The less you eat, drink, buy books, go to the theatre, go dancing, go drinking, think, love, theorise, sing, paint, fence etc., the more you *save* and the greater will become that treasure which neither moths nor maggots can consume – your *capital*. The less you *are*, the less you give expression to your life, the more you *have*, the greater is your *alienated* life and the more you store up of your estranged life.[43]

The contrast that counts is one between sacrificing your life to your capital, offering yourself up idolatrously to dead matter which appears to be alive, and finding oneself forced into a living death that might furnish the conditions for a more general flourishing.

It is axiomatic that men and women must accomplish their emancipation for themselves. It can no more be delegated than the act of dying. The notion of revolution turns on the paradox that what has been reduced by the arrogance of power to a state of inert objectivity is precisely on that account capable of emerging as a new kind of subject. It is its afflictions that compel it to become an agent. Only by living its wretched condition to the full can it hope to annul it, and in doing so to abolish itself. So it is that the Janus-faced beast of antiquity finally finds a home in the modern political sphere. Seen in this light, revolution is a modern version of what the ancient world knew as sacrifice.

ENDNOTES

1 Radical Sacrifice

1. Quoted by Michelle Gellrich, *Tragedy and Theory* (Princeton, NJ, 1988), p. 37.
2. Jamie M. Ferreira, *Love's Grateful Striving: A Commentary on Kierkegaard's 'Works of Love'* (Oxford, 2001), p. 153.
3. See Ronald Dworkin, *Justice for Hedgehogs* (Cambridge, MA, 2011).
4. John Rawls, *A Theory of Justice* (Cambridge, MA, 2005), pp. 3–4.
5. Jürgen Habermas, *Justifications and Applications: Remarks on Discourse Ethics* (Cambridge, MA, 1993), p. 34.
6. See Edward Burnett Tylor, *Primitive Culture* (Cambridge, 2010), vol. 2, chapter 18.
7. Marcel Detienne, 'Culinary Practices and the Spirit of Sacrifice', in Marcel Detienne and Jean-Pierre Vernant (eds), *The Cuisine of Sacrifice among the Greeks* (Chicago, IL, 1989).
8. See David Janzen, *The Social Meanings of Sacrifice in the Hebrew Bible* (Berlin and New York, 2004), p. 3.
9. The phrase is from Nigel Davies, *Human Sacrifice in History and Today* (London, 1981), p. 24.
10. See Gavin Flood, 'Sacrifice as Refusal', in Julia Meszaros and Johannes Zachhuber (eds), *Sacrifice and Modern Thought* (Oxford, 2013).
11. See Giorgio Agamben, *Language and Death* (Minneapolis, MN, and Oxford, 1991), p. 105. S.W. Sykes argues a similar case in his essay 'Sacrifice in the New Testament and Christian Theology', in M.F.C. Bourdillon and M. Fortes (eds), *Sacrifice* (London and New York, 1980), p. 61.
12. See also, for an absorbing, deeply suggestive study, Marcel Hénaff, *The Price of Truth: Gift, Money, and Philosophy* (Stanford, CA, 2010).
13. Max Horkheimer and Theodor Adorno, *Dialectic of Enlightenment* (London, 1997).
14. Alexandre Kojève, *Introduction to the Reading of Hegel: Lectures on the 'Phenomenology of Spirit'* (Ithaca, NY, 1980), p. 19.
15. Bruce Chilton argues against such a universal theory in his 'The Hungry Knife: Towards a Sense of Sacrifice', in M. Daniel Carroll R., David J.A. Clines and Philip

R. Davies (eds), *The Bible in Human Society: Essays in Honour of John Rogerson* (Sheffield, 1995).

16. See Kathryn McClymond, *Beyond Sacred Violence* (Baltimore, MD, 2008), p. 28.
17. Roger T. Beckwith and Martin J. Selman (eds), *Sacrifice in the Bible* (Grand Rapids, MI, 1995), p. 138.
18. Edmund Leach, *Culture and Communication* (Cambridge, 1976), p. 84.
19. For an account of the affair, see Bruce Chilton, *The Temple of Jesus* (University Park, PA, 1992), chapter 6. For the semiotics of gifts, see Jean-Joseph Goux, 'Seneca against Derrida: Gift and Alterity', in E. Wyschogrod et al. (eds), *The Enigma of Gift and Sacrifice* (New York, 2002).
20. See G.D. Kilpatrick, *The Eucharist in Bible and Liturgy* (Cambridge, 1983), esp. Lecture 4.
21. J.H.M. Beattie, 'On Understanding Sacrifice', in Bourdillon and Fortes (eds), *Sacrifice*, p. 37.
22. Henri Hubert and Marcel Mauss, *Sacrifice: Its Nature and Functions* (London, 1964), p. 99.
23. See Burion Mack, 'Introduction: Religion and Ritual', in Robert G. Hamerton-Kelly (ed.), *Violent Origins* (Stanford, CA, 1987), p. 12.
24. Dennis J. Schmidt, *On Germans and Other Greeks: Tragedy and Ethical Life* (Bloomington, IN, 2001), p. 90.
25. Miguel de Beistegui, 'Hegel: Or the Tragedy of Thinking', in Miguel de Beistegui and Simon Sparks (eds), *Philosophy and Tragedy* (London and New York, 2000), p. 27.
26. Walter Burkert, *Homo Necans* (Berkeley, CA, 1983), p. 38.
27. George Heyman, *The Power of Sacrifice* (Washington, DC, 2007), p. xvi.
28. Quoted by Paolo Diego Bubbio, *Sacrifice in the Post-Kantian Tradition* (Albany, NY, 2014), p. 119.
29. Burkert, *Homo Necans*, p. 38.
30. G.W.F. Hegel, *The Phenomenology of Spirit* (Oxford, 1977), p. 19.
31. Quoted by Beistegui, 'Hegel: Or the Tragedy of Thinking', pp. 18–19.
32. For an informative recent study of sacrifice in ancient Greece, see F.S. Naiden, *Smoke Signals for the Gods: Ancient Greek Sacrifice from the Archaic through Roman Periods* (Oxford, 2013).
33. Giorgio Agamben, *Homo Sacer* (Stanford, CA, 1998), p. 114.
34. Ian Bradley, *The Power of Sacrifice* (London, 1995), p. 70.
35. Detienne and Vernant, *The Cuisine of Sacrifice*, p. 3.
36. See Francis Young, *Sacrifice and the Death of Christ* (Philadelphia, PA, 1975), p. 112.
37. Slavoj Žižek and Boris Gunjevic, *God in Pain: Inversions of Apocalypse* (New York, 2012), p. 62.
38. I have written at greater length on these questions in my *Holy Terror* (Oxford, 2005).
39. Burkert, *Homo Necans*, p. 45.
40. James George Frazer, *The Golden Bough, Part 6: The Scapegoat* (London, 1913), p. 411. For a survey of sacrificial practices in a range of different cultures, see Brenda Lewis, *Ritual Sacrifice* (Stroud, 2001).
41. See also Paul Connerton, *The Tragedy of Enlightenment* (Cambridge, 1980).

42. For Jeremiah's repudiation of sacrifice, see Jacob Milgrom, *Studies in Cultic Theology and Terminology* (Leiden, 1983), chapter 10.

43. Max Weber, *Ancient Judaism* (Glencoe, IL, 1952), p. 375.

44. For sacrifice in the Letter to the Hebrews, see F.W. Dillistone, *The Christian Understanding of the Atonement* (Welwyn, 1968).

45. C.F.D. Moule, *The Sacrifice of Christ* (London, 1965), p. 23.

46. Paula Fredriksen, *Jesus of Nazareth, King of the Jews* (London, 2000), p. 209.

47. Robert J. Daly, *Christian Sacrifice* (Washington, DC, 1978), p. 213.

48. Guy G. Stroumsa, *The End of Sacrifice* (Chicago, IL, and London, 2009), p. 59.

49. See Michael Fishbane, 'Aspects of the Transformation of Sacrifice in Judaism', in Roger Beckwith and Martin Selman (eds), *Sacrifice in the Bible* (Grand Rapids, MI, 1995). Ernst Cassirer charts a similar process in the Hindu tradition, arguing that in the evolution from the early Vedas to the Upanishads, the sacrificial gift becomes gradually more inward (*The Philosophy of Symbolic Forms*, New Haven, CT, and London, 1955, vol. 1. p. 224).

50. Quoted by Johannes Zachhuber, 'Modern Discourse on Sacrifice and its Theological Background', in Julia Meszaros and Johannes Zachhuber (eds), *Sacrifice and Modern Thought* (Oxford, 2013), p. 16.

51. See, for example, Chilton, *The Temple of Jesus*, pp. 124 and 133, and Jonathan Klawans, *Purity, Sacrifice, and the Temple* (Oxford, 2006); a definitive account of sacrifice in the Old Testament is to be found in Roland de Vaux's magisterial *Ancient Israel* (London, 1961), Part 4, chapter 10; J. Skinner's *Prophecy and Religion* (Cambridge, 1992) regards sacrifice as irrelevant to the Old Testament, a view rejected by R.E. Clements in his *Prophecy and Covenant* (London, 1965), vol. 2; for an innovative feminist critique of the practice, see Nancy Jay, *Throughout Your Generations Forever: Sacrifice, Religion, and Paternity* (Chicago, IL, and London, 1992).

52. Denys Turner, *Thomas Aquinas: A Portrait* (New Haven, CT, and London, 2013), p. 188.

53. Robert G. Hamerton-Kelly, 'Sacred Violence and the Curse of the Law (Galatians 3:13): The Death of Christ as a Sacrificial Travesty', *New Testament Studies*, vol. 36 (1991), p. 113.

54. For a study of human sacrifice, see Dennis Hughes, *Human Sacrifice in Ancient Greece* (London, 1991). See also Carol Delaney, *Abraham on Trial* (Princeton, NJ, 1998), and Beate Pongratz-Leisten, 'Ritual Killing and Society in the Ancient Near East', in K. Finsterbusch, A. Lange and K.F. Diethard Romheld (eds), *Human Sacrifice in Jewish and Christian Tradition* (Leiden and Boston, 2007).

55. Agamben, *Homo Sacer*, p. 83.

56. John Milbank, 'The Ethics of Self-Sacrifice', *First Things* (March 1999), https://www.firstthings.com/article/1999/03/004-the-ethics-of-self-sacrifice (accessed 30 October 2017).

57. Jean-Luc Nancy, *A Finite Thinking* (London, 2003), p. 51.

58. D.R. Jones, 'Sacrifice and Holiness', in S.W. Sykes (ed.), *Sacrifice and Redemption* (Cambridge, 1991), p. 132.

59. Marie E. Isaacs, *Sacred Space: An Approach to the Theology of the Epistle to the Hebrews* (Sheffield, 1992), p. 92.

60. See Moule, *The Sacrifice of Christ*, p. 23.

61. See Alain Badiou, *Being and Event* (London, 2005).

2 Tragedy and Crucifixion

1. Simon Sparks, 'Fatalities', in Miguel de Beistegui and Simon Sparks (eds), *Philosophy and Tragedy* (London and New York, 2000), p. 203.
2. See G.D. Kilpatrick, *The Eucharist in Bible and Liturgy* (Cambridge, 1983), especially Lecture 4.
3. See Burion Mack, 'Introduction: Religion and Ritual', in W. Burkert et al. (eds), *Violent Origins* (Stanford, CA, 1987).
4. See Robert G. Hamerton-Kelly, 'Sacred Violence and the Curse of the Law' (Galatians 3:13): The Death of Christ as a Sacrificial Travesty', *New Testament Studies*, vol. 36 (1991), p. 113.
5. Henri Hubert and Marcel Mauss, *Sacrifice: Its Nature and Functions* (London, 1964), p. 98.
6. See Peter Szondi, *On Textual Understanding and Other Essays* (Manchester, 1986), pp. 43–55.
7. Friedrich Schlegel, *Lucinda and the Fragments* (Minneapolis, MN, 1972), p. 253.
8. Quoted in Raymond Williams, *Modern Tragedy* (London, 1966), p. 116.
9. See Theodor Adorno, *Noten zur Literatur* (Frankfurt-am-Main, 1974), p. 423.
10. Friedrich Nietzsche, *The Will to Power* (New York, 1967), p. 543.
11. Friedrich Nietzsche, *The Joyful Wisdom* (London, 1910), p. 60.
12. Friedrich Nietzsche, *Twilight of the Idols* and *The Anti-Christ* (London, 1990), p. 134.
13. Ernst Bloch remarks that the language of ransom, credit and debit, when used of the Crucifixion, belongs to 'demonic jurisprudence' (*The Principle of Hope*, Cambridge, MA, 1995, vol. 3, p. 1266).
14. Mary Douglas, *Purity and Danger* (London and New York, 1966), p. 179.
15. See Jürgen Moltmann, *The Crucified God* (Minneapolis, MN, 1993), pp. 150–3.
16. G.K. Chesterton, *The Man Who Was Thursday* (Harmondsworth, 1986), p. 183.
17. C.F.D. Moule, *The Sacrifice of Christ* (London, 1965), p. 28.
18. Eric L. Santner, 'Miracles Happen', in S. Žižek, E. Santner and K. Reinhardt (eds), *The Neighbour: Three Inquiries in Political Theology* (Chicago, IL, 2005), p. 120.
19. See Slavoj Žižek and Boris Gunjevic, *God in Pain: Inversions of Apocalypse* (New York, 2012), pp. 55–6.
20. See Slavoj Žižek, *The Ticklish Subject* (London, 1999), p. 161, and *The Fragile Absolute* (London, 2000), chapter 4.
21. See Alain Badiou, *Saint Paul: The Foundations of Universalism* (Stanford, CA, 2003), p. 71.
22. Jacques Derrida, *The Gift of Death* (Chicago, IL, and London, 1996), pp. 96–7. For an impressively erudite account of Abraham's summons to kill Isaac, see Larry Powell and William R. Self, *Holy Murder* (Lanham, MD, 2007).
23. Herbert McCabe, OP, *Hope* (London, 1987), p. 4.
24. Jean-Luc Marion, *The Crossing of the Visible* (Stanford, CA, 2004), p. 54.
25. Søren Kierkegaard, *Fear and Trembling* and *Repetition* (Princeton, NJ, 1983), p. 60.
26. A claim made by Gavin Flood in Meszaros and Zachhuber (eds), *Sacrifice and Modern Thought*, p. 128.
27. Bloch, *The Principle of Hope*, vol. 3, p. 1172.
28. See Terry Eagleton, *On Evil* (New Haven, CT, and London, 2010), chapter 2.
29. See G.W.F. Hegel, *Early Theological Writings* (Philadelphia, PA, 1971), p. 261.
30. See Robin Lane Fox, *Pagans and Christians* (Harmondsworth, 1986), p. 70.

31. Carlin Barton, 'Honor and Sacredness in the Roman and Christian Worlds', in Margaret Cormack (ed.), *Sacrificing the Self* (Oxford, 2002), p. 30.
32. Ibid., p. 29.
33. Fred Botting and Scott Wilson (eds), *The Bataille Reader* (Oxford, 1997), p. 210.
34. Ibid., p. 212.
35. See Michael Richardson (ed.), *Georges Bataille: Essential Writings* (London, 1998), p. 62.
36. Nigel Davies, *Human Sacrifice in History and Today* (London, 1981), pp. 3 and 20.
37. See Lane Fox, *Pagans and Christians*, pp. 37ff.
38. Marcel Detienne and Jean-Pierre Vernant, *The Cuisine of Sacrifice among the Greeks* (Chicago, IL, 1989), pp. 3–4 and 20.
39. Beattie in M.F.C. Bourdillon and M. Fortes (eds), *Sacrifice* (London and New York, 1980), p. 34.
40. Girard develops his case in (among other places) *The Scapegoat* (Baltimore, MD, 1986), *Things Hidden since the Foundation of the World* (Stanford, CA, 1987) and *I See Satan Fall Like Lightning* (Maryknoll, NY, 1999); for an equally negative case about sacrifice, see Jean-Pierre Dupuy, *La marque du sacré* (Paris, 2008).
41. See, for example, Wolfgang Palaver's notably emollient treatment of Girard's work in his otherwise valuable study *René Girard's Mimetic Theory* (East Lansing, MI, 2013), pp. 240–5.
42. See René Girard, 'Generative Scapegoating', in Robert G. Hamerton-Kelly (ed.), *Violent Origins* (Stanford, CA, 1987), p. 142. Hamerton-Kelly's Introduction to the volume ventures scarcely a single substantial criticism of Girard's work. As such, for all their undoubted insights, these texts are typical of a body of commentary on Girard's ideas that exudes a distinct air of hagiography.
43. Rowan Williams levels this criticism at Girard in his 'Between Politics and Metaphysics: Reflections in the Wake of Gillian Rose', in M. Higton (ed.), *Wrestling with Angels: Conversations in Modern Theology* (London, 2007), pp. 10–11.
44. René Girard, *Things Hidden Since the Foundation of the World* (Stanford, CA, 1987), p. 214.
45. John Milbank, 'Stories of Sacrifice', *Contagion: Journal of Violence, Mimesis, and Culture*, 2 (1995).

3 Martyrdom and Mortality

1. Montaigne, *Essays* (Harmondsworth, 1979), p. 329. Sidney Axinn defines sacrifice as the giving of a gift without expectation of return, and regards this as the source of all intrinsic value. See his *Sacrifice and Value* (Lanham, MD, 2010), especially chapter 2.
2. See Samuel Scheffler, *Death and the Afterlife* (Oxford, 2013), p. 86.
3. Thomas Nagel raises some difficulties about this so-called deprivation theory of the fear of death in *Mortal Questions* (Cambridge, 1979), pp. 4–10.
4. Ibid., p. 2.
5. Thomas Nagel, *The View from Nowhere* (New York and Oxford, 1986), p. 228.
6. See Bernard Williams, 'The Makropulos Case: Reflections on the Tedium of Immortality', in *Problems of the Self* (Cambridge, 1973).
7. Ibid., p. 94. Nagel also overlooks the distinction between eternity and infinity, and so does Shelly Kagan in his *Death* (New Haven, CT, and London, 2012), chapter 11.

8. John Macquarrie, *Christian Hope* (London and Oxford, 1978), p. 19.
9. Scheffler, *Death and the Afterlife*, pp. 108 and 11.
10. The words are in fact Niko Kolodny's, in his Introduction to Scheffler's study (ibid., p. 10).
11. Stephen Mulhall, *Faith and Reason* (London, 1994), p. 65.
12. Ludwig Wittgenstein, *Tractatus Logico-Philosophicus* (London, 1961), 6.431.
13. See Gianni Vattimo, *The End of Modernity* (Cambridge, 1991), chapter 7.
14. Slavoj Žižek, *Living in the End Times* (London, 2010), p. 307.
15. Quentin Meillassoux, *After Finitude* (London, 2008), p. 57.
16. Though Jean-Yves Lacoste, a disciple of Heidegger, upbraids the master for an excessive emphasis on the appropriation of one's death as a strenuous accomplishment. See his *Experience and the Absolute: Disputed Questions on the Humanity of Man* (Fordham, NY, 2004), p. 62.
17. Immanuel Kant, *Religion within the Limits of Reason Alone* (New York, 1960), p. 126.
18. Walter Benjamin, *The Origin of German Tragic Drama* (London, 1963), p. 114.
19. William Desmond, *Perplexity and Ultimacy* (New York, 1995), p. 53.
20. See Jacques Derrida, 'Donner la mort', in J.-M. Rabate and M. Wetzel (eds), *L'Ethique du don* (Paris, 1992).
21. Nagel, *Mortal Questions*, p. 11.
22. Maurice Blanchot, *The Siren's Song* (Brighton, 1982), p. 149.
23. Jean-Joseph Goux, *Oedipus, Philosopher* (Stanford, CA, 1993), p. 184.
24. Theodor Adorno, *Minima Moralia* (London, 1974), p. 227.
25. Ernst Bloch, *The Principle of Hope* (Cambridge, MA, 1995), vol. 3, p. 1105.
26. Tacitus, *The Annals* (Oxford, 2008), p. 97.
27. Benjamin, *The Origin of German Tragic Drama*, p. 114.
28. Herbert McCabe, OP, *Hope* (London, 1987), p. 24.
29. See Martin Heidegger, *Being and Time*, 7th edn, trans. John Macquarrie and Edward Robinson (New York, 1962), p. 243.
30. See Terry Eagleton, *Trouble with Strangers: A Study of Ethics* (Oxford, 2009), part 3.
31. Montaigne, *Essays*, p. 401.
32. See Robin Lane Fox, *Pagans and Christians* (Harmondsworth, 1986), p. 442.
33. Quoted by Arthur J. Droge and James D. Tabor, *A Noble Death: Suicide and Martyrdom among Christians and Jews in Antiquity* (New York, 1992), p. 169; see also Brad S. Gregory, *Salvation at Stake* (Cambridge, MA, and London, 1999), chapter 4.
34. See Slavoj Žižek and Boris Gunjevic, *God in Pain: Inversions of Apocalypse* (New York, 2012), p. 51.
35. David Wood, *The Step Back: Ethics and Politics after Deconstruction* (Albany, NY, 2005), p. 89; for a theological account of martyrdom, see Nicholas Lash, 'What Might Martyrdom Mean?', in W. Horbury and B. McNeill (eds), *Suffering and Martyrdom in the New Testament* (Cambridge, 1981).
36. Robin Young, *In Procession before the World: Martyrdom as Public Liturgy in Early Christianity* (Milwaukee, WI, 2001), p. 10.
37. Benjamin, *The Origin of German Tragic Drama*, p. 109.
38. Henri Hubert and Marcel Mauss, *Sacrifice: Its Nature and Functions* (London, 1964), p. 100.

39. John Milbank, *The Future of Love* (London, 2009), p. 359.
40. One may note, however, that the Christian Eucharist is a common meal which establishes conviviality through a communal participation in the sacrifice of Calvary, and to this extent founds its symbolic order on a deathly encounter with the Real. Self-sacrifice and abundance of life here coincide, rather than the former being a condition of the latter.
41. John Milbank, 'The Ethics of Self-Sacrifice', *First Things* (March 1999), https://www.firstthings.com/article/1999/03/004-the-ethics-of-self-sacrifice (accessed 30 October 2017).
42. Jean-Luc Marion, *The Crossing of the Visible* (Stanford, CA, 2004), p. 54.
43. Hubert and Mauss, *Sacrifice: Its Nature and Functions*, p. 101.
44. See Thomas Hobbes, *Leviathan* (Cambridge, 2010), p. 94.
45. See Alain Badiou, *Ethics: An Essay on the Understanding of Evil* (London, 2001).
46. Jacques Lacan, *The Four Fundamental Principles of Psychoanalysis* (London, 1977), pp. 275–6.
47. See Lawrence Fine, 'Contemplating Death in Jewish Mystical Tradition', in M. Cormack (ed.), *Sacrificing the Self* (Oxford, 2002).
48. Martin Heidegger, *Being and Time* (New York, 1966), p. 231.
49. Giorgio Agamben, *Language and Death* (Minneapolis, MN, and Oxford, 1991), p. 2.
50. Heidegger, *Being and Time*, p. 232.
51. Ibid., p. 244. I refer to Donne's claim in his *Devotions upon Emergent Occasions* that every death somehow involves the whole of humanity: 'any man's death diminishes me, because I am involved in mankind'.
52. For a critique of Heidegger on death, see Jean-Luc Nancy, *Being Singular Plural* (Stanford, CA, 2000), pp. 88–91.
53. Quoted by Malcolm Bull, *Anti-Nietzsche* (London, 2011), p. 112.
54. Simon Critchley, *Ethics-Politics-Subjectivity* (London, 1999), p. 222.
55. See Charles Taylor, *Sources of the Self* (Cambridge, 1989), part 3.
56. For an excessively positive reading of the poem, see Terence [*sic*] Eagleton, *The New Left Church* (London and Melbourne, 1966), pp. 24–5.
57. Jacques Derrida, *The Gift of Death* (Chicago, IL, and London, 1996), p. 97.
58. Ibid., p. 101.
59. Ibid., p. 107.
60. Paul Ricoeur, *Essays on Biblical Interpretation* (Philadelphia, PA, 1980), p. 164.
61. René Girard, *Quand ces choses commenceront* (Paris, 1994), p. 76.
62. Bloch, *The Principle of Hope*, vol. 3, p. 1263. Bloch writes perceptively on the eschatological nature of Christian ethics in this volume of his work.
63. Wittgenstein, *Tractatus Logico-Philosophicus*, 6.4311.

4 Exchange and Excess

1. Jacques Derrida, *Given Time: I. Counterfeit Money* (Chicago, IL, and London, 1992), p. 12.
2. John Milbank, *Being Reconciled: Ontology and Pardon* (London, 2003), p. 181.
3. See Guy G. Stroumsa, *The End of Sacrifice* (Chicago, IL, and London 2009), pp. 68–9.
4. McKenzie Wark, *The Beach Beneath the Street* (London and New York, 2011), p. 72.
5. See Jean-Joseph Goux, 'Seneca against Derrida: Gift and Alterity', in E. Wyschogrod et al. (eds), *The Enigma of Gift and Sacrifice* (New York, 2002), p. 134.

6. Seneca, *Moral Essays*, vol. 2 (Cambridge, MA, and London, 2006), p. 161.
7. Derrida, *Given Time*, p. 29.
8. See on this point Jacques T. Godbout and Alain Caille, *The World of the Gift* (Montreal, 1998), pp. 185f.
9. John Milbank, 'The Ethics of Self-Sacrifice', *First Things* (March 1999), https://www.firstthings.com/article/1999/03/004-the-ethics-of-self-sacrifice (accessed 30 October 2017).
10. See John Milbank, 'Can a Gift be Given? Prolegomena to a Future Trinitarian Metaphysics', in L.G. Jones and S.E. Fowl (eds), *Rethinking Metaphysics* (Oxford, 1995). See also his *The Future of Love* (London, 2009), p. 357.
11. For a valuable account, see Paul Mason, *PostCapitalism: A Guide to Our Future* (London, 2015).
12. Kevin Hart (ed.), *Counter-Experiences: Reading Jean-Luc Marion* (Notre Dame, IN, 2007), p. 37. John Caputo is another who confuses reciprocity with economic exchange. See his 'The Time of Giving, the Time of Forgiving', in Wyschogrod et al. (eds), *The Enigma and Gift of Sacrifice*.
13. Hart (ed.), *Counter-Experiences*, p. 37.
14. John Milbank, 'The Gift and the Mirror: On the Philosophy of Love', in ibid., p. 262.
15. See in particular Jean-Luc Marion, *Le phénomène érotique: Six méditations* (Paris, 2003); see also his *Being Given: Towards a Phenomenology of Givenness* (Stanford, CA, 2002).
16. F.D. Kidner, *Sacrifice in the Old Testament* (London, 1952), p. 23.
17. Alain Badiou, *Saint Paul: The Foundations of Universalism* (Stanford, CA, 2003), p. 78.
18. Marcel Hénaff, *The Price of Truth: Gift, Money, and Philosophy* (Stanford, CA, 2010), pp. 107f. Bernard S. Cohen argues that some Europeans in seventeenth- and eighteenth-century India regularly misinterpreted the exchange of gifts as a contractual affair. See his *Colonialism and its Forms of Knowledge* (Princeton, NJ, 1996), pp. 18–19.
19. Hénaff, *The Price of Truth*, p. 141.
20. Oliver Goldsmith, 'Justice and Generosity', in A. Friedman (ed.), *Collected Works of Oliver Goldsmith* (Oxford, 1966), vol. 2.
21. R.B. McDowell (ed.), *Writings and Speeches of Edmund Burke* (Oxford, 1991), vol. 9, p. 247.
22. See Marcel Mauss, *The Gift* (London, 1990).
23. See Seneca, *Moral Essays*, vol. 2, p. 20.
24. See Carlin Barton, 'Honor and Sacredness in the Roman and Christian Worlds', in Margaret Cormack (ed.), *Sacrificing the Self* (Oxford, 2002), p. 26.
25. Maurice Godelier, *The Enigma of the Gift* (Cambridge, 1999), p. 30.
26. See Milbank, 'Can a Gift be Given?', p. 120.
27. Quentin Meillassoux, *After Finitude* (London, 2009), p. 63.
28. Ian Bradley, *The Power of Sacrifice* (London, 1995), p. 132.
29. Stephen Mulhall, *Faith and Reason* (London, 1994), p. 60.
30. See Wark, *The Beach Beneath the Street*, pp. 70–2.
31. Derrida, *Given Time*, p. 24.
32. Godelier, *The Enigma of the Gift*, p. 30.
33. Carlin A. Barton, *Roman Honor: The Fire in the Bones* (Berkeley, CA, 2001), p. 238.

34. Goux, 'Seneca against Derrida', p. 149.

35. Fred Botting and Scott Wilson (eds), *The Bataille Reader* (Oxford, 2010), p. 68.

36. See Friedrich Nietzsche, *Thus Spake Zarathustra* (London, 2003), p. 281.

37. See Milbank, *Being Reconciled*, pp. 44–7.

38. See E.P. Sanders, *Jesus and Judaism* (London, 1985), p. 271; for an erudite exposition of the Pauline view of the gift, see John M.G. Barclay, *Paul and the Gift* (Grand Rapids, MI, and Cambridge, 2015).

39. Jean-Luc Nancy, *Adoration: The Deconstruction of Christianity II* (New York, 2013), p. 14.

40. See Alain Badiou, *Being and Event* (London, 2005).

41. Adrian Poole, *Tragedy: A Very Short Introduction* (Oxford, 2005), p. 35.

42. Georges Bataille, *The Accursed Share* (New York, 1988), vol. 1, p. 59.

43. Most critical commentary on the novel adopts a decidedly angelic view of its heroine. See, for one instance among many, Dorothea Krook, *The Ordeal of Consciousness in Henry James* (Cambridge, 1962), chapter 7.

44. Godelier, *The Enigma of the Gift*, p. 12.

45. See William Davies, *The Happiness Industry* (London, 2016), p. 182.

46. Ibid., p. 185.

5 Kings and Beggars

1. For an account of the scapegoat in classical antiquity, see Dennis D. Hughes, *Human Sacrifice in Ancient Greece* (London, 1991), chapter 5; and Jean-Pierre Vernant and Pierre Vidal-Naquet, *Myth and Tragedy in Ancient Greece* (New York, 1990), chapter 5; for the Hebrew scapegoat ritual of the Day of Atonement, see George Buchanan Gray, *Sacrifice in the Old Testament* (New York, 1971), chapter 20.

2. Jean-Joseph Goux, *Oedipus, Philosopher* (Stanford, CA, 1993), pp. 184–5.

3. Arthur Schopenhauer, *The World as Will and Representation* (New York, 1969), vol. 1, pp. 378–9.

4. John Haffenden, *William Empson, vol. 1: Among the Mandarins* (Oxford, 2005), p. 384.

5. William Empson, *Some Versions of Pastoral* (Harmondsworth, 1966), p. 20; see also William Righter, 'Fool and *Pharmakon*', in C. Norris and N. Mapp (eds), *William Empson: The Critical Achievement* (Cambridge, 1993).

6. René Girard, *Violence and the Sacred* (London, 2013), p. 120.

7. Jacques Derrida, *Dissemination* (Chicago, IL, 1981), p. 133.

8. William Robertson Smith, *Lectures on the Religion of the Semites* (Sheffield, 1995), p. 10.

9. James George Frazer, *The Golden Bough, Part 6: The Scapegoat* (London, 1913), p. 143.

10. I have discussed some of these questions before, in my *Sweet Violence: The Idea of the Tragic* (Oxford, 2003), chapter 10, and *Holy Terror* (Oxford, 2005), chapter 6.

11. Giorgio Agamben, *Language and Death* (Minneapolis, MN, and Oxford, 1991), p. 105.

12. Jürgen Moltmann, *Theology of Hope* (London, 1967), p. 32 (translation amended).

13. Vernant and Vidal-Naquet, *Myth and Tragedy in Ancient Greece*, p. 106.

14. Mary Douglas, *Purity and Danger* (London and New York, 1966), p. 168.

15. It is possible, however, to see the Eucharist as combining all three Lacanian dimensions of imaginary, symbolic and Real. If it involves the Real, it is also a matter of an 'imaginary' exchange of identities, as each member of the community donates herself in the gift of bread and wine and receives the others back in the same medium. It is also a symbolic order in itself. See Terry Eagleton, *Trouble with Strangers: A Study of Ethics* (Oxford, 2009), pp. 195–6 and 323.

16. Edmund Leach, *Culture and Communication* (Cambridge, 1976), p. 83.

17. See Terry Eagleton, *On Evil* (New Haven, CT, and London, 2010), chapter 2.

18. Giorgio Agamben, *Remnants of Auschwitz* (New York, 1999), p. 63.

19. Walter Benjamin, *Understanding Brecht* (London, 1973), p. 57.

20. Agamben, *Remnants of Auschwitz*, p. 33.

21. For some reflections on these questions, see Eric L. Santner, 'Miracles Happen', in S. Žižek, E. Santner and K. Reinhardt (eds), *The Neighbour: Three Inquiries in Political Theology* (Chicago, IL, 2005).

22. Agamben, *Remnants of Auschwitz*, p. 77.

23. Dorothy Van Ghent, *The English Novel: Form and Function* (New York, 1953), p. 136.

24. Douglas, *Purity and Danger*, p. 168.

25. Ibid., p. 6.

26. Agamben, *Language and Death*, p. 105.

27. Slavoj Žižek, *Living in the End Times* (London, 2010), p. 116.

28. René Girard, *The Scapegoat* (Baltimore, MD, 1986), p. 33.

29. See Julia Kristeva, *Powers of Horror* (New York, 1982), pp. 65–6.

30. See Jacques Rancière, *Aux bords du politique* (Paris, 1998), p. 38.

31. Malcolm Bull, *Seeing Things Hidden* (London, 1999), p. 79.

32. Girard, *The Scapegoat*, p. 42.

33. See George Heyman, *The Power of Sacrifice* (Washington, DC, 2007), p. 133.

34. See Vernant and Vidal-Naquet, *Myth and Tragedy in Ancient Greece*, p. 103.

35. See Jacques Derrida, *The Beast and the Sovereign* (Chicago, IL, and London, 2009).

36. Søren Kierkegaard, *The Sickness Unto Death* (London, 1989), p. 100.

37. Girard, *Violence and the Sacred*, p. 267.

38. Carl Schmitt, *Political Theology: Four Chapters on the Concept of Sovereignty* (Chicago, IL, 2006).

39. Slavoj Žižek, quoted by I. Parker in *Slavoj Žižek: A Critical Introduction* (London, 2004), p. 150.

40. Vernant and Vidal-Naquet, *Myth and Tragedy in Ancient Greece*, p. 139.

41. Quoted by D. Dennis Hudson, 'Self-Sacrifice as Truth in India', in M. Cormack (ed.), *Sacrificing the Self* (Oxford, 2002), p. 132.

42. Karl Marx, *An Introduction to the Critique of Hegel's 'Philosophy of Right'* (Cambridge, 1970), pp. 141–2 (translation amended).

43. Ibid., p. 361.

INDEX